Acid Reflux Diet Cookbook

Tame the Flames of Heartburn with Hundreds of Flavorful, GERD & LPR-Friendly Recipes

9 Secret Tips to Experience the Relief You Deserve without Sacrificing Taste

Betty Karen Taylor

Table of Contents

Introduction

Gastric reflux can be a real pain, especially if not properly managed. The good news is that there are many delicious meals that can help you reduce symptoms and improve your health. This recipe book is just for you, packed with a wide range of healthy and delicious recipes that will make your mouth water. You may find simple to follow recipes for breakfast, lunch, dinner, and snacks using everyday products.

In addition, you'll learn how to modify your eating habits to reduce gastric reflux symptoms. For example, you'll avoid foods that can worsen symptoms like spicy and fatty foods and choose foods that can help soothe esophagus irritation like leafy green vegetables and rice.

The book will also teach you what to eat and when to eat to avoid overloading your stomach and causing reflux. It will help you to avoid eating too much at one time and to avoid lying down right after eating.

Finally, I hope this recipe book will help you manage gastric reflux symptoms in a fun and tasty way. I am confident that with this cookbook you will be able to prepare tasty and healthy meals that will help you manage your gastric reflux symptoms and improve your quality of life. Enjoy your meal!

An Overview on Gastroesophageal Reflux

Acid reflux, also known as gastroesophageal reflux, is a disorder in which stomach acid goes back into the esophagus, producing heartburn, chest pain, and swallowing trouble. Numerous things, such as nutrition, way of life, and underlying medical issues, can lead to acid reflux.

Diet plays an essential role in managing acid reflux. There are some products that can worsen or cause reflux symptoms by increasing acid production in the stomach. Additionally, there are certain foods that can help reduce symptoms of reflux, such as fruits and vegetables, whole grains, low-fat milk and dairy, fish and poultry.

To manage acid reflux, it is important to avoid eating fatty and spicy foods, limit consumption of coffee, alcohol and citrus fruits, and eat smaller, more frequent meals instead of large meals. It is also important to avoid eating before bedtime and lying down immediately after eating to prevent acid from flowing back into the esophagus.

Moreover, some studies have shown that following a low-carb diet can help manage acid reflux symptoms as this kind of diet can reduce acid production in the stomach.

To manage acid reflux, it is vital to eat a well-balanced diet. This means choosing healthy and nutrient-rich foods, avoiding fatty and spicy foods, and limiting consumption of coffee, alcohol and citrus fruits. Additionally, it is important to avoid eating before bedtime and lying down immediately after eating to prevent acid from flowing back into the esophagus.

What is Acid Reflux?

Gastroesophageal reflux disease, also known as GERD, is a chronic and often debilitating condition that affects millions of people worldwide. It is defined by the backward movement of stomach contents into the esophagus, including acid and other digestive enzymes. This backflow can cause a wide range of symptoms, including heartburn, chest pain, sore throat, hoarseness, and difficulty swallowing. The main causes of acid reflux are a malfunctioning lower esophageal sphincter (LES) and a hiatal hernia. The lower esophageal sphincter (LES) is a muscle that links the esophagus to the stomach and normally contracts to prevent stomach acid from leaking back into the esophagus. If the LES is compromised or loosened, stomach acid can flow into the esophagus, resulting in acid reflux symptoms. A hiatal hernia occurs when the top of the stomach pushes through the diaphragm and into the chest cavity. This can weaken the LES and increase the likelihood of stomach acid flowing back into the esophagus. Hiatal hernias are more common in older adults, and they can be caused by factors such as obesity, pregnancy, and heavy lifting.

Certain foods and beverages might also cause acid reflux symptoms. These include spicy foods, fried foods, citrus fruits, chocolate, caffeine, and alcohol. Eating large meals or close to bedtime may also raise the risk of acid reflux. Obesity, which increases pressure on the stomach and LES, can also contribute to acid reflux. Smokers are also more likely to experience acid reflux because smoking can weaken the LES and cause damage to the esophagus. Acid reflux symptoms can also be caused by medications such as nonsteroidal anti-inflammatory drugs (NSAIDs), blood pressure medications, and antidepressants. If you've been taking any of these medications and suffering acid reflux symptoms, talk to your doctor about possible alternatives.

In some cases, acid reflux may be caused by an underlying medical condition such as Gastroesophageal Reflux Disease (GERD) which is a chronic form of acid reflux, or a Helicobacter pylori infection. A doctor should identify and treat these illnesses.

Acid reflux can be caused by a wide range of variables, including a dysfunctional lower esophageal sphincter, a hiatal hernia, certain meals and beverages, obesity, smoking, and certain drugs.

Symptoms

Heartburn, which feels like a burning feeling rising from the stomach to the esophagus, is one of the most prevalent symptoms of acid reflux. Common symptoms include chest pain, difficulty swallowing, belching, nausea, coughing, and hoarseness. Some people with acid reflux may also experience a feeling of choking or a sour taste in the mouth. Acid reflux can also cause complications such as inflammation of the esophagus (esophagitis), formation of ulcers in the esophagus (peptic ulcer) and a condition called Barrett's esophagus, in which the cells of the esophagus change due to chronic exposure to acid.

Risk factors

There are some risk factors that can increase the likelihood of developing acid reflux, including obesity, smoking, use of certain medications, pregnancy and some medical conditions such as hiatal hernia and Gastroesophageal reflux disease (GERD).

If you suspect you have acid reflux, go to a doctor for a diagnosis. The doctor can perform a series of tests to determine if symptoms are caused by acid reflux, including a physical exam, an x-ray of the esophagus, an endoscopy and a pH-metry.

To manage symptoms of acid reflux, the doctor may recommend changes in diet and lifestyle, such as avoiding fatty and spicy foods, limiting consumption of coffee, alcohol and citrus fruits, and eating smaller, more frequent meals instead of large meals. In the event of serious symptoms or issues, a physician may prescribe drugs to reduce stomach acid. With proper diagnosis and treatment, symptoms of acid reflux can be managed and quality of life improved. Antacids, H2 receptor blockers, and proton pump inhibitors are examples of over-the-counter drugs that can be used to treat GERD symptoms. These drugs, however, only provide short-term comfort and do not address the underlying source of the disease. In more severe cases, a procedure called fundoplication may be performed to strengthen the LES and prevent stomach contents from refluxing into the esophagus.

It is vital to note that GERD can progress to major consequences such as esophagitis, Barrett's esophagus, and even esophageal cancer if left untreated.

What to Eat

While there is no one-size-fits-all diet for those with acid reflux, certain foods can help to reduce symptoms and promote overall health. The following is a list of 10 foods that are recommended for those with acid reflux, due to their low acidity and other beneficial properties.

1. Leafy greens: Leafy greens such as spinach, kale, and lettuce are low in acid and high in fiber, making them a great option for those with acid reflux. They also contribute in the neutralization of stomach acid and the promotion of healthy digestion.

2. Bananas: Bananas are a great option for those with acid reflux because they are low in acid and high in potassium. Potassium contributes in the neutralization of stomach acid and can help to alleviate acid reflux symptoms.

3. Oatmeal: Due to its high fiber content and ability to absorb stomach acid, oatmeal is an excellent choice for those suffering from acid reflux. It also improves digestion and can help in the relief of acid reflux symptoms.

4. Lean proteins: Lean proteins such as chicken, fish, and turkey are low in fat and easy to digest, which can help to reduce acid reflux symptoms. They also give the body vital nutrients that promote general health.

5. Root vegetables: Root vegetables such as potatoes, sweet potatoes, and carrots are low in acid and high in fiber. They are also easy to digest and contribute to reducing acid reflux symptoms.

6. Non-citrus fruits: Non-citrus fruits such as apples, berries, and melons are low in acid and high in fiber. They also promote good digestion and can help in the alleviation of acid reflux symptoms.

7. Ginger: Ginger has natural anti-inflammatory properties and can help to reduce acid reflux symptoms. It can be taken as tea, supplement, or mixed with food.

8. Almond milk: Almond milk is a great option for those with acid reflux because it is low in acid and can help to neutralize stomach acid. It also improves digestion and helps in the relief of acid reflux symptoms.

9. Yogurt: Yogurt is an excellent choice for people who suffer from acid reflux because it contains probiotics, which assist to balance the gut microbiota and support good digestion.

10. Healthy fats: Healthy fats such as avocado, olive oil, and nuts are easy to digest and can help to reduce acid reflux symptoms. They are also a source of vital nutrients that promote general health.

What Foods to Avoid

What you eat can be just as essential as what you don't eat when it comes to acid reflux management. Certain foods have been known to aggravate acid reflux symptoms and should be avoided in order to keep symptoms under control. The following are ten foods that are generally recognized to aggravate acid reflux symptoms.

- Fried and fatty foods: Fried and fatty foods can increase stomach acid production and relax the lower esophageal sphincter, resulting in acid reflux symptoms. Foods such as French fries, fried chicken, and fatty meats should be avoided.
- Tomato-based products: Tomatoes and tomato-based products are high in acid, which can aggravate acid reflux symptoms. Foods such as pizza, marinara sauce, and salsa should be avoided.
- Spicy foods: Spicy foods can irritate the esophageal membrane and increase acid production in the stomach, leading to acid reflux symptoms. Hot peppers, curry, and chili should all be avoided.
- Garlic and onions: Garlic and onions can irritate the esophageal membrane and increase acid production in the stomach, resulting in acid reflux symptoms.
- Caffeine and other stimulants in chocolate can relax the lower esophageal sphincter, enabling stomach acid to flow back into the esophagus.
- Peppermint: Peppermint can relax the lower esophageal sphincter, enabling stomach acid to return to the esophagus.

It's important to note that some people with acid reflux may have unique food triggers, so it's always a good idea to monitor your own body's reaction to different types of food.

What to Drink

If you have gastroesophageal reflux disease (GERD), it's important to be mindful of what you drink as well as what you eat. Certain beverages can make your symptoms worse, while others can assist to alleviate them. If you have GERD, here are some general tips regarding what to drink and what to avoid:

1. Water: The finest beverage for satisfying thirst and rehydrating your body is water. It's also alkaline, which can improve the neutralization of stomach acid. Drinking water can also be useful to wash out any acid that has refluxed into the esophagus, which can alleviate symptoms. Drink at least 8 glasses of water per day.
2. Low-fat milk or non-dairy alternatives: These can provide a source of calcium and other nutrients, but choose low-fat options to avoid aggravating GERD symptoms. Milk can also help to neutralize stomach acid, providing relief. Non-dairy alternatives such as almond or soy milk are also good options, but be sure to avoid those that are sweetened or flavored.
3. Herbal tea: Some herbal teas, such as ginger, chamomile, or licorice, may help to soothe the digestive system and reduce inflammation. Ginger in particular has been found to have anti-inflammatory properties and can help to reduce the symptoms of GERD.
4. Decaffeinated coffee or tea: Caffeine can aggravate GERD symptoms, so it's best to avoid it. However, some people can tolerate decaffeinated coffee or tea without experiencing symptoms. It's important to monitor your own personal tolerance.

What Drinks to Avoid

- Alcohol relaxes the lower esophageal sphincter, allowing stomach acid to return to the esophagus. It can also cause an increase in symptoms by stimulating acid production in the stomach. To reduce GERD symptoms, restrict or limit your alcohol consumption.
- Carbonated drinks: The bubbles in carbonated drinks can cause stomach distention, which can trigger reflux. Carbonated beverages can also increase acid production in the stomach, causing symptoms to worsen.
- Citrus juices: These can be high in acid and can irritate the esophagus. The acidity in citrus juices can also stimulate acid production in the stomach, leading to increased symptoms.
- Coffee and tea with caffeine: As mentioned earlier, caffeine can aggravate GERD symptoms. It's best to avoid it, or limit your intake to minimize symptoms.

Best Tips and Tricks to Avoid Gastric Reflux

1. Avoid spicy, greasy, and fatty foods: These types of foods can increase acid production in the stomach and worsen acid reflux symptoms. The lower esophageal sphincter may also relax as a result, enabling stomach acid to flow back into the esophagus.
2. Eat small, frequent meals instead of large meals: Eating smaller, more frequent meals can help reduce the amount of acid in the stomach and prevent acid reflux. Large meals can lead the stomach to create more acid, which can then reflux into the esophagus.
3. Avoid eating close to bedtime: Eating close to bedtime can cause acid reflux symptoms to worsen as gravity is not helping keep stomach contents where they should be. When we lie down, it makes it easier for stomach acid to flow back into the esophagus, so it's best to avoid eating for at least 2-3 hours before going to bed.
4. Elevate the head of your bed: Elevating the head of your bed can help reduce nighttime acid reflux by allowing gravity to keep stomach contents where they should be. This can be accomplished by placing blocks below the bed's foot or by utilizing a foam wedge pillow.
5. Try to maintain a healthy weight: Being overweight can increase the risk of acid reflux, so try to maintain a healthy weight to reduce symptoms. Extra weight puts strain on the stomach, causing acid to run back into the esophagus.
6. Cook with low-acid ingredients such as vegetables and lean proteins: Cooking with low-acid ingredients can help reduce acid reflux symptoms as they are less likely to aggravate the condition. Some examples of low-acid foods include leafy greens, broccoli, asparagus, lean meats, fish, and poultry.
7. Avoid alcohol and caffeine: Both can relax the lower esophageal sphincter, allowing stomach acid to flow back into the esophagus. They also increase stomach acid production, which can aggravate acid reflux symptoms.
8. Chew your food thoroughly: Chewing your food thoroughly can help to reduce the amount of acid needed to digest it. This can help prevent acid reflux symptoms from occurring.

9. Watch your medications: Certain medications such as anti-inflammatory drugs, calcium channel blockers, and antidepressants can relax the lower esophageal sphincter and increase the risk of acid reflux. If you are using any of these medications, please check with your doctor about possible alternatives.

10. Use stress-relief techniques: Stress can increase stomach acid production and relax the lower esophageal sphincter, both of which can cause acid reflux symptoms. Try relaxation techniques like yoga or meditation to relieve tension.

Breakfasts

Blueberry Almond Smoothie

Preparation Time: 5 minutes
Cooking Time: 5 minutes
Servings: 1
Ingredients:

- ½ cup almond milk
- 1 cup blueberries, frozen
- 1 apple
- 1 pitted date
- 1 piece fresh ginger root
- ¼ tsp turmeric, ground
- pinch of pink Himalayan salt

Directions:
1. In a blender, blend all ingredients until very smooth. Enjoy!

Nutrition: Calories: 397 kcal; **Total Fat:** 6.2 g; **Total Carbohydrates:** 82.4 g; **Protein:** 9.6 g

Low Fat Greek Yogurt with Acai Berry Granola

Preparation Time: 5 minutes
Cooking Time: 5 minutes
Servings: 2
Ingredients:

- 2 cups nonfat Greek yogurt
- 2 tsp raw honey
- ½ cup granola cereal
- ½ cup acai berries, frozen

Directions:
1. Pour the yogurt into a serving bowl or a glass and stir in raw honey and top with granola, sprinkle acai berries on top. Enjoy!

Nutrition: Calories: 230 kcal; **Total Fat:** 18.2 g; **Total Carbohydrates:** 45.5 g; **Protein:** 29.1 g

Ginger and Turmeric Detox Tea

Preparation Time: 10 minutes
Cooking Time: 20 minutes
Servings: 2
Ingredients:

- 6 bags green tea
- 2 cups water
- 1 cup fresh ginger, chopped
- 3 cinnamon sticks
- 1 tsp turmeric, ground

Directions:
1. Add chopped ginger and green tea bags to a pan of water and bring to a rolling boil.
2. Lower heat and simmer for about 10 minutes.
3. Add in turmeric, and cinnamon stick, and cook for another 10 minutes. remove the pan from heat and let cool before straining.
4. Refrigerate for at least 1 hour or until chilled.

Nutrition: Calories: 194 kcal; **Total Fat:** 3.9 g; **Total Carbohydrates:** 37.1 g; **Protein:** 4.2 g

Simple Steel-Cut Oats

Preparation Time: 15 minutes or fewer
Cooking Time: 6 to 8 hours on warm
Servings: 4–6
Ingredients:

- ½ tbsp coconut oil
- 4 cups boiling water
- ½ tsp sea salt
- 1 cup steel-cut oats

Directions:
1. Coat the slow cooker with coconut oil.
2. In your slow cooker, combine the boiling water, salt, and oats.

3. Cover the cooker and set it to warm (or low if there is no warm setting). Cook for 6 to 8 hours and serve.

Cleanup tip: I wouldn't typically recommend using the warm temperature setting on your slow cooker as a go-to cooking solution, but for steel-cut oats, it creates a better texture with less mess, as the oats will boil and leave hard-to-clean residue on the high setting. Just make sure the water you use is boiling when you add it in at the start.

Nutrition: Calories: 172 kcal; **Total Fat:** 6 g; **Total Carbohydrates:** 27 g; **Sugar:** 0 g; **Fiber:** 4 g; **Protein:** 6 g; **Sodium:** 0.29 g

Sour Cherry and Pumpkin Seed Granola

Preparation Time: 10 minutes
Cooking Time: 5 to 6 hours on low
Servings: 4–6
Ingredients:
- 1 tbsp coconut oil, melted and divided
- 1 cup unsweetened coconut, shredded
- 1 cup rolled oats
- 1 cup pecans
- ½ cup pumpkin seeds
- 1 ripe banana
- 1 tbsp vanilla extract
- ½ tsp sea salt
- ½ tsp cinnamon, ground
- ½ tsp ginger, ground
- 1 cup sour cherries, dried

Directions:
1. Coat the slow cooker with 1 tbsp of coconut oil.
2. In your slow cooker, toss together the coconut, oats, pecans, and pumpkin seeds.
3. In a small bowl, mash the banana with the remaining ¼ cup of melted coconut oil, vanilla, salt, cinnamon, and ginger.
4. Add the liquid ingredients to the granola mixture and stir well to combine.
5. Cover the cooker and set it to low. Cook for 5 to 6 hours (see Tip).

6. When the cooking is finished, stir in the cherries.
7. Spread the granola on a flat surface or baking sheet to cool and dry completely before storing it in airtight containers. Stored in a cool place, this will keep up to six months.

Important cooking tip: To get crispy granola, it must lose its moisture in the cooking process. I usually don't recommend lifting the lid during the cooking time, but in this case, you can leave the lid slightly ajar the entire cook time to vent condensation, or fit a dishtowel between the slow cooker and its lid to absorb condensation.

Nutrition: Calories: 777 kcal; **Total Fat:** 18 g; **Total Carbohydrates:** 58 g; **Sugar:** 25 g; **Fiber:** 10 g; **Protein:** 7 g; **Sodium:** 0.30 g

Active Weight Loss Tea

Preparation Time: 10 minutes
Cooking Time: 1 hour 20 minutes
Servings: 2
Ingredients:
- 4 cups hot water
- 1-inch ginger root, thinly sliced
- 2 cinnamon sticks
- 4 green tea bags

Directions:
1. Add the hot water to a large pot over high heat and add the cinnamon stick and sliced ginger. Bring to a boil then turn off the heat. Add the tea bags and let the tea steep.
2. You can drink this tea as is or sweeten it with some raw honey.
3. Sip on this tea first thing in the morning, before your breakfast, and the last thing before you sleep for maximum fat-burning benefits.

Nutrition: Calories: 47 kcal; **Total Fat:** 1.2 g; **Total Carbohydrates:** 7.5 g; **Protein:** 1.3 g

Healthy Amaranth Porridge

Preparation Time: 10 minutes
Cooking Time: 40 minutes
Servings: 2

Ingredients:
- ½ cup amaranth
- 1 ½ cups water
- ¼ cup almond milk
- 1 tsp stevia
- ¼ tsp sea salt

Directions:
1. In a pan, combine water, salt, and amaranth and bring to a boil; cover and simmer for about 30 minutes and then stir in milk and stevia and cook, stirring until the porridge is creamy. Serve right away.

Nutrition: Calories: 190 kcal; **Total Fat:** 3.8 g; **Total Carbohydrates:** 27.7 g; **Protein:** 7.3 g

Buckwheat Pancakes with Elderberries

Preparation Time: 10 minutes
Cooking Time: 16 minutes
Servings: 4
Ingredients:
- 1 tsp coconut oil
- 1 cup almond milk
- 1 cup buckwheat flour, ground
- ¼ tsp turmeric powder
- 1 tsp salt
- ½ inch ginger, grated
- 1 handful cilantro, chopped
- 1 cup fresh elderberries to serve

Directions:
1. In a bowl, combine buckwheat, almond milk, and spices until well combined; stir in cilantro, and ginger until well blended.
2. Melt coconut oil in a saucepan over medium-low heat; add about one-quarter of a cup of batter and spread out on the pan.
3. Cook the pancakes for about 4 minutes per side or until golden brown. Transfer to a plate and keep warm; repeat with the remaining batter and oil.
4. Top the pancakes with fresh elderberries and fold them into wraps. Serve with a glass of freshly squeezed orange juice.

Nutrition: Calories: 386 kcal; **Total Fat:** 6.3 g; **Total Carbohydrates:** 20.5 g; **Protein:** 4.1 g

Fruity Detox Tea

Preparation Time: 10 minutes
Cooking Time: 1 hour 20 minutes
Servings: 1
Ingredients:
- 2 cucumber slices
- 2 strawberries, thinly sliced
- 1 green tea bag
- 1 tsp raw honey
- 1 cup boiling water

Directions:
1. Add the tea bag to the cup of water and let steep until it cools completely. Stir in all the remaining ingredients and you are ready to drink.
2. You can add some ice cubes if you like your tea super chilled.

Nutrition: Calories: 49 kcal; **Total Fat:** 0.2 g; **Total Carbohydrates:** 12 g; **Protein:** 0.9 g

Superfood Overnight Oats

Preparation Time: 10 minutes
Cooking Time: 0 minutes
Servings: 2
Ingredients:
- ½ cup old-fashioned oats
- 1 tsp chia seeds
- ½ cup vanilla almond milk, unsweetened
- ¼ cup fresh blueberries
- ¼ banana, chopped
- ¼ cup fresh pineapple, chopped
- ¼ cup nonfat Greek yogurt
- ¼ tsp cinnamon

Directions:

1. In a small jar, combine oats, chia seeds, almond milk, blueberries, banana, pineapple, yogurt, and cinnamon. Refrigerate overnight.
2. To serve, remove from the fridge and stir to mix well before serving.

Nutrition: Calories: 310 kcal; **Total Fat:** 8.4 g; **Total Carbohydrates:** 29 g; **Protein:** 10.8 g

Omelet

Preparation Time: 10 minutes
Cooking Time: 10 minutes
Servings: 2
Ingredients:

- 1 tsp olive oil
- 1 small zucchini, chopped
- 2 eggs
- ½ tsp turmeric powder
- 2 tbsp coriander, chopped
- Salt to taste

Directions:
1. In a bowl, combine coriander, and turmeric powder until well blended; whisk in the eggs and season with salt and pepper.
2. In a skillet, heat oil and then pour in about a third of the mixture; swirl the pan to spread the egg mixture and cook for about 1 minute per side or until the egg is set.
3. Transfer to a plate and keep warm. Repeat with the remaining mixture. Serve hot with orange juice or chai for a satisfying breakfast meal.

Nutrition: Calories: 241 kcal; **Total Fat:** 7.4 g; **Total Carbohydrates:** 6.2 g; **Protein:** 9.2 g

Healthy Buckwheat, Millet, and Amaranth Porridge

Preparation Time: 10 minutes
Cooking Time: 30 minutes
Servings: 4
Ingredients:

- ½ cup buckwheat groats
- ½ cup whole grain amaranth
- ½ cup whole grain millet
- 5 cups water
- 1 tsp kosher salt
- 1 tbsp flax seeds
- 2 cups almond milk
- 1 tsp cinnamon, ground
- ⅛ tsp nutmeg, ground
- 2 tbsp raw honey

Directions:
1. Rinse the grains and add to a pot of boiling salted water; lower heat and simmer for about 30 minutes or until the grains are cooked through.
2. Remove from heat and stir in almond milk; divide among serving bowls and drizzle each serving with raw honey and sprinkle with cinnamon and nutmeg. Enjoy!

Nutrition: Calories: 318 kcal; **Total Fat:** 3.4 g; **Total Carbohydrates:** 55.7 g; **Protein:** 9.5 g

Ginger Almond Berry Smoothie Bowl

Preparation Time: 10 minutes
Cooking Time: 0 minutes
Servings: 2

Ingredients:
- 1 cup unsweetened almond milk
- 1 scoop vanilla protein powder
- 1 tbsp flaxseed, ground
- 1 cup kale, chopped
- 1 tsp fresh ginger, minced
- 1 cup spinach, frozen, chopped
- 1 cup blueberries
- 1 cup strawberries

Directions:
1. Combine all ingredients in a blender and blend until very smooth and creamy. Divide the smoothie between serving bowls and top each with your favorite toppings. Enjoy!

Nutrition: Calories: 222 kcal; **Total Fat:** 8.2 g; **Total Carbohydrates:** 8.1 g; **Protein:** 3.7 g

Citrus Turmeric Smoothie

Preparation Time: 5 minutes
Cooking Time: 5 minutes
Servings: 2
Ingredients:
- 1 tsp turmeric
- ½ orange, segmented
- 1 cup Greek yogurt
- ½ cup mango chunks
- ½ cup almond milk
- 1 banana, sliced

Directions:
1. Blend all ingredients until very smooth. Enjoy!

Nutrition: Calories: 209 kcal; **Total Fat:** 3.8 g; **Total Carbohydrates:** 32.8 g; **Protein:** 13.6 g

Chai Spiced Greek Yogurt Parfait with Fresh Fruits

Preparation Time: 10 minutes
Cooking Time: 0 minutes
Servings: 4

Ingredients:
- 1 cup granola cereal
- 2 cups non-fat Greek yogurt
- ½ tsp allspice, ground
- ½ tsp ginger, ground
- ½ tsp cardamom, ground
- ½ tsp cloves, ground
- ½ tsp nutmeg, ground
- ½ tsp cinnamon, ground
- 1 banana, sliced
- 1 cup apricots, halved

Directions:
1. In a small bowl, stir together yogurt and spices until well combined.
2. Sprinkle a small layer of granola in a serving glass and then top with a layer of yogurt mixture followed by banana slices and apricot halves; repeat the layers to fill the glasses.
3. Enjoy!

Nutrition: Calories: 207 kcal; **Total Fat:** 8.4 g; **Total Carbohydrates:** 48.6 g; **Protein:** 20.2 g

Mushrooms, Boiled Eggs, and Veggie Breakfast Bowl

Preparation Time: 5 minutes
Cooking Time: 10 minutes
Servings: 2
Ingredients:
- 4 large boiled eggs, diced
- 1 tsp extra-virgin olive oil
- ½ cup button mushrooms, chopped
- 1 cup arugula/baby spinach

Directions:
1. Heat olive oil in a pan set over medium heat; add mushrooms and sauce for about 5 minutes or until tender.
2. Stir in arugula and cook for about 5 minutes or until it wilts; add diced boiled eggs and cook for a few minutes.

Nutrition: Calories: 201 kcal; **Total Fat:** 6.8 g; **Total Carbohydrates:** 4.4 g; **Protein:** 13.9 g

Egg Frittata

Preparation Time: 10 minutes
Cooking Time: 10 minutes
Servings: 4
Ingredients:

- 5 eggs
- 1 tsp paprika
- ½ tsp salt
- 1 tbsp cilantro, chopped
- 1 cup zucchini, diced
- 1 tbsp coconut oil

Directions:

1. Preheat your oven to 350°F.
2. Whisk together eggs, spices, and cilantro in a bowl; set aside.
3. Heat oil in a skillet and then stir salt for 2 minutes; add in zucchini and cook, covered, for 10 minutes or until zucchini are soft.
4. Add in the egg mixture and stir in to combine. Cook for about 5 minutes and then transfer to the oven. Bake for about minutes or until the egg is set.

Nutrition: Calories: 164 kcal; **Total Fat:** 1.9 g; **Total Carbohydrates:** 6.3 g; **Protein:** 7.9 g

Wholesome Buckwheat Pancakes

Preparation Time: 10 minutes
Cooking Time: 10 minutes
Servings: 2
Ingredients:

- ⅔ cup raw buckwheat groats, soaked overnight, and rinsed
- 1 egg
- ¼ tsp cinnamon
- 1 tsp stevia
- ¼ tsp sea salt
- ½ cup water

Directions:

1. Transfer rinsed and drained buckwheat to a blender and add in egg, stevia, cinnamon, salt, and water and blend until very smooth.
2. Grease a nonstick skillet and set over medium heat; pour in about a third cup of the buckwheat batter, spreading to cover the bottom of the skillet.
3. Cook for about 2 minutes over the side until the pancake is golden brown. Repeat with the remaining batter.
4. Serve right away with a glass of orange juice.

Nutrition: Calories: 166 kcal; **Total Fat:** 3.5 g; **Total Carbohydrates:** 26.4 g; **Protein:** 7.8 g

Healthy Brown Rice Breakfast Bowl

Preparation Time: 10 minutes
Cooking Time: 10 minutes
Servings: 4
Ingredients:

- 2 cups brown rice, cooked
- ½ cup unsweetened almond milk
- 1 tsp liquid stevia
- 1 tbsp almond butter
- 1 apple, diced
- 2 dates, chopped
- ½ tsp cinnamon

Directions:

1. Combine almond oil, almond butter, stevia, apple, and dates in a saucepan; bring to a gentle boil and then cook for

about 5 minutes or until the apples are tender; stir in cinnamon and brown rice and cook for about 5 minutes and then remove from heat.

2. Serve immediately.

Nutrition: Calories: 226 kcal; **Total Fat:** 4.3 g; **Total Carbohydrates:** 4.3 g; **Protein:** 5.8 g

Oats with Berries

Preparation time: 10 minutes
Cooking time: 30 minutes
Servings: 4
Ingredients:

- 1 cup Steel Cut Oats
- Dash of Salt
- 3 cups Water
- For toppings:
- ½ cup Berries of your choice
- ¼ cup Nuts or Seeds of your choice like Almonds or Hemp Seeds

Directions:

1. To begin with, place the oats in a small saucepan and heat it over medium-high heat.
2. Now, toast it for 3 minutes while stirring the pan frequently.
3. Next, pour water to the saucepan and mix well.
4. Allow the mixture to boil. Lower the heat.
5. Allow it to cook for 23 to 25 minutes or until the oats are cooked and tender.
6. Once done cooking, transfer the mixture to the serving bowl and top it with the berries and seeds.
7. Serve it warm or cold.
8. Tip: If you desire, you can add sweeteners like maple syrup or coconut sugar or stevia to it.

Nutrition: Calories: 118Kcal; Protein: 4.1g; Carbohydrates: 16.5g; Fat: 4.4g;

Golden Beet and Spinach Frittata

Preparation Time: 15 minutes or fewer
Cooking Time: 5 to 7 hours on low
Servings: 4–6
Ingredients:

- 1 tbsp extra-virgin olive oil
- 8 large eggs
- 1 cup packed fresh spinach leaves, chopped
- 1 cup golden beets, diced and peeled
- ¼ cup unsweetened almond milk
- ¾ tsp sea salt
- ½ tsp basil leaves, dried
- Black pepper, freshly ground

Directions:

1. Coat the slow cooker with olive oil.
2. In a large bowl, combine the eggs, spinach, beets, almond milk, salt, and basil, and season with pepper. Whisk together and pour the custard into the slow cooker.
3. Cover the cooker and set it to low. Cook for 5 to 7 hours, or until the eggs are completely set, and serve.

Storage tip: This frittata should keep in the refrigerator for up to 3 days. Keep in mind that overheating the frittata to warm it could cause the eggs to become rubbery.

Nutrition: Calories: 202 kcal; **Total Fat:** 14 g; **Total Carbohydrates:** 6 g; **Sugar:** 4 g; **Fiber:** 1 g; **Protein:** 13 g; **Sodium:** 0.60 g

Perfect Hard-Boiled Eggs

Preparation Time: 15 minutes or fewer
Cooking Time: 2 ½ hours on high
Servings: 6
Ingredients:

- 6 large eggs
- 1 tbsp distilled white vinegar

Directions:

1. Place the eggs along the bottom of the slow cooker, making sure none are stacked.
2. Add enough water to the slow cooker to just cover the eggs. Add the vinegar.
3. Cover the cooker and set it to high. Cook for 2½ hours. Let cool before serving.

Preparation tip: Gently place the eggs in a bowl of ice water as soon as the cooking time is up to make them even easier to peel.
Nutrition: Calories: 74 kcal; **Total Fat:** 5 g; **Total Carbohydrates:** 1 g; **Sugar:** 1 g; **Fiber:** 0 g; **Protein:** 6 g; **Sodium:** 0.70 g

Cauliflower Quiche

Preparation Time: 10 minutes
Cooking Time: 26 minutes
Servings: 4
Ingredients:

- ½ head cauliflower, chopped
- ½ tsp salt
- ½ cup almond milk
- 1 cup baby spinach
- 4 eggs
- 1 cup pitted olives, chopped or sliced
- 3 cup water
- 1 tbsp olive oil

Directions:

1. Make sure you steam the cauliflower first. You can do that with your Instant pot and a little help from the steaming basket. Pour a cup of water into the pot then place the steaming basket with cauliflower.
2. Seal the lid and set it to Manual, cooking for 4 minutes on High pressure. Release the pressure and safely remove the lid and the steaming basket. Next, whisk in eggs with almond milk, baby spinach, and salt.
3. Combine with steamed cauliflower. Use 4 ramekins to distribute the mixture you have made and pour the remaining 3 cups of water into the pot. Place the trivet and then arrange the ramekins covered with tin foil.
4. Seal the lid and set the pot to Manual, cooking for 12 minutes. Release pressure naturally for 10 minutes. Serve with olives.

Nutrition: Calories: 176 kcal; **Fat:** 5 g; **Protein:** 17 g; **Carbohydrates:** 8 g

Spinach Omelet

Preparation Time: 5 minutes
Cooking Time: 5 minutes
Servings: 1
Ingredients:

- 2 eggs
- 60 g. spinach leaves
- Salt (to taste)

Directions:

1. Add your eggs and spinach together in a medium bowl, season with salt, and pepper, and whisk to combine. Set a lightly greased skillet over medium heat and allow it to get hot.
2. Add egg mixture, once hot, and cook until egg begins to set (about 3 min). Flip your egg over halfway to form an omelet and continue to cook until fully set (about another 2 mins). Enjoy!

Nutrition: Calories: 161 kcal; **Fat:** 10 g; **Protein:** 13 g; **Carbohydrates:** 6 g

Spinach and Egg Bites

Preparation Time: 45 minutes
Cooking Time: 12 minutes
Servings: 4
Ingredients:

- 1 cup spinach, roughly chopped.
- 2 cup shitake mushrooms, chopped
- ½ cup uncooked millet
- 2 cup water
- 6 eggs
- 1 cup coconut milk
- ½ tsp salt
- ½ cup Nutritional yeast
- 1 tsp turmeric

Directions:

1. Set the oven to preheat to 350°F. Lightly grease your muffin tin. Toast millet over medium heat, stirring occasionally.
2. Add water and salt, cover, and switch to high heat allowing to boil. Decrease the heat slightly and continue cooking until the water is absorbed. In a small bowl, whisk eggs, coconut milk, salt, and turmeric.
3. Toss together with millet, spinach, and mushrooms; mix very well. Spoon into muffin cups; bake 10 to 12 minutes, or until lightly firm to the touch. Sprinkle with Nutritional yeast as soon as the egg bites come out of the oven; allow it to cool slightly before serving.

Nutrition: Calories: 412 kcal; **Fat:** 8 g; **Protein:** 29 g; **Carbohydrates:** 34 g

Roasted Superfood Vegetables Frittata

Preparation Time: 20 minutes
Cooking Time: 1 hour and 15 minutes
Servings: 6
Ingredients:

- 3 medium red bell peppers, remove and discard seeds, slice into quarters
- Nonstick cooking spray
- 2 large zucchinis, sliced into 3–½-inch strips
- 1 tbsp olive oil
- 1 tsp salt
- ¼ cup fresh parsley, chopped
- 4 eggs plus 6 egg whites

Directions:

1. Prepare the oven to 425°F. Arrange the oven racks so that one is at the lowest position and another is in the middle. Take 2 baking pans with shallow bottoms. Line with foil. Spray the surface lightly with cooking spray. Put the bell pepper in one of the prepared baking pans.
2. Place zucchini in the other pan. Spray the vegetables lightly with some of the cooking sprays. Place the pan with the zucchini on the lower oven rack.
3. Place the other pan on the center oven rack. Roast the vegetables for 15 minutes. Remove the pans and change the positions on the oven. Place the pan with the zucchini on the center rack and the other pan on the lower rack. Roast for another 10 minutes, until the vegetables are charred.
4. Remove the pans from the oven and set aside for 5 minutes. Lower the oven temperature to 350°F. Remove the skins from the peppers. Chop everything coarsely. Put in a mixing bowl.
5. Add ½ tsp salt and parsley. Mix. Lightly grease the bottom of a 9-inch round baking pan.

6. Put eggs and egg whites in a mixing bowl, season with the remaining salt, and then whisk thoroughly.
7. Pour the egg mixture over the vegetables. Pour the entire mixture into the prepared round pan. Bake in 350°F oven for 45 to 50 minutes. Once the center has set, remove the frittata from the oven. Let the frittata rest for about 5 minutes so it can set. Slice and serve while still warm.

Nutrition: Calories: 139 kcal; **Fat:** 7 g; **Protein:** 31 g; **Carbohydrates:** 18 g

Spinach Avocado Smoothie

Preparation time: 5 minutes
Cooking time: 5 minutes
Servings: 1
Ingredients:
- ¼ of 1 Avocado
- 1 cup Plain Yoghurt, non-Fat:
- 2 tbsp. Water
- 1 cup Spinach, fresh
- 1 tsp. Honey
- 1 Banana, frozen

Directions:
1. Start by blending all the ingredients needed to make the smoothie in a high-speed blender for 2 to 3 minutes or until you get a smooth and creamy mixture.
1. Next, transfer the mixture to a serving glass.
2. Serve and enjoy.

Tip: If you don't prefer to use yogurt, you can use unsweetened almond milk.

Nutrition: Calories: 357Kcal; Protein: 7.7g; Carbohydrates: 37.8g; Fat: 8.2g

Golden Milk

Preparation time: 5 minutes
Cooking time: 5 minutes
Servings: 2
Ingredients:
- 1 tbsp. Coconut Oil
- 1 ½ cups Coconut Milk, light
- Pinch of Pepper
- 1 ½ cups Almond Milk, unsweetened
- ¼ tsp. Ginger, grated
- 1 ½ tsp. Turmeric, grounded
- ¼ tsp. Cinnamon, grounded
- Sweetener of your choice, as needed

Directions:
1. To make this healthy beverage, you need to place all the ingredients in a medium-sized saucepan and mix it well.

3. After that, heat it over medium heat for 3 to 4 minutes or until it is hot but not boiling. Stir continuously.
4. Taste for seasoning. Add more sweetener or spice as required by you.
5. Finally, transfer the milk to the serving glass and enjoy it.

Tip: Instead of cinnamon powder, you can also use the cinnamon stick, which can be discarded at the end if you prefer a much more intense flavor.

Nutrition: Calories: 205Kcal; Protein: 3.2g; Carbohydrates: 8.9g; Fat: 19.5g

Granola

Preparation time: 10 minutes
Cooking time: 60 minutes
Servings: 2
Ingredients:
- ½ cup Flax Seeds, grounded
- 1 cup Almonds, whole & raw
- ½ cup Ginger, grated
- 1 cup Pumpkin Seeds, raw
- ½ tsp. Salt
- 1 cup Shredded Coconut, unsweetened
- ¾ cup Water
- 1 cup Oat Bran
- ½ cup Coconut Oil, melted
- 1 cup Dried Cherries, pitted
- 4 tsp. Turmeric Powder

Directions:
1. First, preheat the oven to 300 deg. F.
2. Next, combine dried cherries, almonds, grounded flax, pumpkin seeds, coconut, salt, and turmeric in a large mixing bowl until mixed well.
3. After that, mix ginger, coconut oil, and water in the blender and blend for 30 to 40 seconds or until well incorporated.
4. Now, spoon in the coconut oil mixture to the nut mixture. Mix well.

5. Then, transfer the mixture to a parchment paper-lined baking sheet and spread it across evenly.
6. Bake for 50 to 60 minutes while checking on it once or twice.
7. Allow it to cool completely and enjoy it.

Tip: Substitute dried cherries with raisins if preferred.

Nutrition: Calories: 225Kcal; Protein: 6g; Carbohydrates: 18g; Fat: 16g

Overnight Coconut Chia Oats

Preparation time: 10 minutes
Cooking time: 60 minutes
Servings: 1 to 2
Ingredients:
- ½ cup Coconut Milk, unsweetened
- 2 tsp. Chia Seeds
- 1 ½ cups Old Fashioned Oats, whole grain
- ½ tsp. Cinnamon, grounded
- 1 cup Almond Milk, unsweetened
- ½ tsp. Cinnamon, grounded
- 2 tsp. Date Syrup
- ½ tsp. Black Pepper, grounded
- 1 tsp. Turmeric, grounded

Directions:
1. To start with, keep the oats in the mason jar.
2. After that, mix the rest of the ingredients in a medium bowl until combined well.
3. Then, pour the mixture to the jars and stir well.
4. Now, close the jar and place it in the refrigerator overnight.
5. In the morning, stir the mixture and then enjoy it.

Tip: You can top it with toasted nuts or berries.

Nutrition: Calories: 335Kcal; Protein: 8g; Carbohydrates: 34.1g; Fat: 19.9g

Blueberry Hemp Seed Smoothie

Preparation time: 10 minutes
Cooking time: 5 minutes
Servings: 1
Ingredients:
- 1 ¼ cup Blueberries, frozen
- 1 ¼ cup Plant-Based Milk of your choice
- 2 tbsp. Hemp Seeds
- 1 tsp. Spirulina
- 1 scoop of Protein: Powder

Directions:

1. First, place all the ingredients needed to make the smoothie in a high-speed blender and blend them for 2 minutes or until smooth.
2. Transfer the mixture to a serving glass and enjoy it.

Tip: Instead of blueberries, you can use any berries of your choice.

Nutrition: Calories: 493Kcal; Protein: 37.8g; Carbohydrates: 46.3g; Fat: 19.6g

Chia Pudding with Oats, Strawberries, and Kiwi

Preparation time: 25 minutes
Cooking time: 0 minutes
Servings: 2
Ingredients:
- 2 cups unsweetened almond milk
- 1 cup chia seeds
- ¼ cup maple syrup
- ½ teaspoon vanilla extract
- ½ cup toasted oats
- 4 large strawberries, sliced
- 1 kiwi, peeled and sliced

Directions:
1. In a quart-size jar with a tight-fitting lid, combine the milk, chia seeds, maple syrup, and vanilla. Cover and shake well, then set aside for at least 15 minutes for the pudding to thicken. (This can even be done the night before and refrigerated overnight.)
2. Divide the pudding between two serving dishes, top with the toasted oats, strawberries, and kiwi, and serve.

Nutrition: Calories: 360Kcal; Protein: 8g; Carbohydrates: 60g; Fat: 11g

Spiced Morning Chia Pudding

Preparation time: 10 minutes
Cooking time: 5 minutes
Servings: 1

Ingredients:
- ½ tsp. Cinnamon
- 1 ½ cups Cashew Milk
- 1/8 tsp. Cardamom, grounded
- 1/3 cup Chia Seeds
- 1/8 tsp. Cloves, grounded
- 2 tbsp. Maple Syrup
- 1 tsp. Turmeric

Directions:
1. To begin with, combine all the ingredients in a medium bowl until well mixed.
2. Next, spoon the mixture into a container and allow it to sit overnight.
3. In the morning, transfer to a cup and serve with toppings of your choice.

Tip: You can top it with toppings of your choice like coconut flakes or seeds etc.

Nutrition: Calories: 237Kcal; Protein: 8.1g; Carbohydrates: 28.9g; Fat: 8.1g

Gingerbread Oatmeal

Preparation time: 10 minutes
Cooking time: 30 minutes
Servings: 4
Ingredients:
- ¼ tsp. Cardamom, grounded
- 4 cups Water
- ¼ tsp. Allspice
- 1 cup Steel Cut Oats
- 1/8 tsp. Nutmeg
- 1 ½ tbsp. Cinnamon, grounded
- ¼ tsp. Ginger, grounded
- ¼ tsp. Coriander, grounded
- Maple Syrup, if desired
- ¼ tsp. Cloves

Directions:
1. Place all ingredients in a huge saucepan over medium-high heat and stir well.
2. Next, cook them for 6 to 7 minutes or until cooked.

3. Once finished, add the maple syrup.
4. Top it with dried fruits of your choice if desired.
5. Serve it hot or cold.
6. Tip: Avoid those spices which you don't prefer.

Nutrition: Calories: 175Kcal; Protein: 6g; Carbohydrates: 32g; Fat: 32g

Roasted Almonds

Preparation time: 5 minutes
Cooking time: 10 minutes
Servings: 20
Ingredients:
- 2 cups whole almonds
- ½ teaspoon ground cinnamon
- ½ teaspoon ground cumin
- ½ teaspoon ground coriander
- Salt and freshly ground black pepper, to taste
- 1 tablespoon extra-virgin organic olive oil

Directions:
1. Preheat the oven to 350 deg. F. Line a baking dish with a parchment paper.
2. In a bowl, add all ingredients and toss to coat well.
3. Transfer the almond mixture into prepared baking dish in a single layer.
4. Roast for around 10 minutes, flipping twice inside the middle way.
5. Remove from oven and make aside to cool down the completely before serving.
6. You can preserve these roasted almonds in airtight jar.

Nutrition: Calories: 62Kcal; Protein: 5g; Carbohydrates: 12g; Fat: 7g

Delicate Rice with Coconut and Berries

Preparation time: 10 minutes
Cooking time: 30 minutes
Servings: 4

Ingredients:
- 1 cup water
- 1 cup coconut milk
- 1 teaspoon salt
- 2 dates, pitted and chopped
- 1 cup blueberries, or raspberries, fresh and divided
- ¼ cup slivered almonds, toasted and divided
- ½ cup coconut, shaved and divided

Directions:
1. Combine the basmati rice, water, coconut milk, salt, and date pieces in a medium saucepan over high heat.
6. Stir until the mixture comes to a boil. For 20 to 30 minutes, lower the heat to simmer and cook, without stirring, or until the rice is tender.
7. Divide the rice among four bowls and top each serving with ¼ cup of blueberries, 1 tablespoon of almonds, and 2 tablespoons of coconut.

Nutrition: Calories: 281Kcal; Protein: 6g; Carbohydrates: 49g; Fat: 6g

Roasted Pumpkin Seeds

Preparation time: 10 minutes
Cooking time: 20 minutes
Servings: 4
Ingredients:
- 1 cup pumpkin seeds, washed and dried
- 2 teaspoons garam masala
- ¼ teaspoon ground turmeric
- Salt, to taste
- 3 tablespoons coconut oil, meted

Directions:
1. Preheat the oven to 350 deg. F.
2. In a bowl, add all ingredients and toss to coat well.
3. Transfer the almond mixture right into a baking sheet.
4. Roast approximately twenty or so minutes, flipping occasionally.
5. Remove from oven and make aside to cool completely before serving.

Nutrition: Calories: 136Kcal; Protein: 12g; Carbohydrates: 9g; Fat: 14g

Spiced Popcorn

Preparation time: 5 minutes
Cooking time: 2 minutes
Servings: 2-3
Ingredients:
- 1 tablespoons coconut oil

- ½ cup popping corn
- 1 teaspoon ground turmeric
- Salt, to taste

Directions:
1. In a pan, melt coconut oil on medium-high heat.
2. Add popping corn and cover the pan tightly.
3. Cook, shaking the pan occasionally for around 1-2 minutes or till corn kernels begin to pop.
4. Remove from heat and transfer right into a large heatproof bowl.
5. Add essential spices and mix well.
6. Serve immediately.

Nutrition: Calories: 200Kcal; Protein: 4g; Carbohydrates: 12g; Fat: 4g

Cucumber Bites

Preparation time: 15 minutes
Cooking time: 0 minutes
Servings: 4
Ingredients:
- ½ cup prepared hummus
- 2 teaspoons nutritional yeast
- ¼-½ teaspoon ground turmeric
- Pinch of red pepper cayenne
- Pinch of salt
- 1 cucumber, cut diagonally into ¼-½-inch thick slices
- 1 teaspoon black sesame seeds
- Fresh mint leaves, for garnishing

Directions:
1. In a bowl, mix together hummus, turmeric, cayenne and salt.
2. Transfer the hummus mixture in the pastry bag and spread on each cucumber slice.
3. Serve while using garnishing of sesame seeds and mint leaves.

Nutrition: Calories: 203Kcal; Protein: 8g; Carbohydrates: 14g; Fat: 5g

Crispy Chicken Fingers

Preparation time: 15 minutes
Cooking time: 18 minutes
Servings: 4-6
Ingredients:

- 2/3 cup almond meal
- ½ teaspoon ground turmeric
- ½ teaspoon paprika
- Salt and freshly ground black pepper, to taste
- 1 egg
- 1-pound skinless, boneless chicken breasts, cut into strips

Directions:

1. Preheat the oven to 375 deg. F. Line a substantial baking sheet with parchment paper.
2. In a shallow bowl, beat the egg.
3. In another shallow dish, mix together almond meal and spices.
4. Coat each chicken strip with egg after which roll into spice mixture evenly.
5. Arrange the chicken strips onto prepared baking sheet in the single layer.
6. Bake for approximately 16-18 minutes.

Nutrition: Calories: 236Kcal; Protein: 37g; Carbohydrates: 26g; Fat: 10g

Cold Oatmeal with Apple and Cinnamon

Preparation time: 10 minutes
Cooking time: 10 minutes
Servings: 4-6
Ingredients:

- 1 cups coconut milk
- ¼ cup no-added-sugar apple juice
- 1 tablespoon apple cider vinegar
- 1 apple, cored and chopped
- Dash ground cinnamon

Directions:

3. Stir together the oats, coconut milk, apple juice, and vinegar in a medium bowl.
8. Cover and refrigerate overnight.

9. Stir in the chopped apple and season the cold oatmeal with cinnamon the next morning.

Nutrition: Calories: 213Kcal; Protein: 6g; Carbohydrates: 39g; Fat: 4g

Beautiful Buckwheat Waffles

Preparation time: 15 minutes
Cooking time: 6 minutes
Servings: 4
Ingredients:

- 1½ cups buckwheat flour
- ½ cup brown rice flour
- 2 teaspoons baking powder
- 1 teaspoon baking soda
- ½ teaspoon sea salt
- 1 egg
- 1 tablespoon maple syrup
- 2 teaspoons vanilla extract
- 1 cup water
- 1½ cups almond milk
- Coconut oil

Directions:

1. Whisk together the buckwheat flour, rice flour, baking powder, baking soda, and salt in a medium bowl.
2. Add the egg, maple syrup, and vanilla to the dry ingredients. Slowly whisk in the water and almond milk until the batter is completely smooth.
3. Let the batter sit for 10 minutes to thicken slightly.
4. Stir well before using because the buckwheat may settle in the bottom of the bowl while resting.
5. Heat the waffle iron and brush it with coconut oil.
6. Add the batter to the waffle iron and cook.

Nutrition: Calories: 282Kcal; Protein: 9g; Carbohydrates: 55g; Fat: 4g

Appetizing Crepes with Berries

Preparation time: 15 minutes
Cooking time: 5 minutes
Servings: 4-6
Ingredients:

- 1 cup buckwheat flour
- ½ teaspoon sea salt
- 2 tablespoons coconut oil (1 tablespoon melted)
- 1½ cups almond milk, or water
- 1 egg
- 1 teaspoon vanilla extract
- 3 cups fresh berries, divided
- 6 tablespoons Chia Jam, divided

Directions:

1. Whisk together the buckwheat flour, salt, 1 tablespoon of melted coconut oil, almond milk, egg, and vanilla in a small bowl until smooth.
2. Melt the remaining 1 tablespoon of coconut oil in a large (12-inch) nonstick skillet over medium-high heat. Tilt the pan, coating it evenly with the melted oil.
3. Into the skillet, ladle ¼ cup of batter. Tilt the skillet to coat it evenly with the batter.
4. Cook for 2 minutes, or until the edges begin to curl up. Flip the crêpe and cook for 1 minute on the second side using a spatula. Transfer the crêpe to a plate.
5. Continue to make crêpes with the remaining batter. You should have 4 to 6 crêpes.
6. Place 1 crêpe on a plate, top with ½ cup of berries and 1 tablespoon of Chia Jam. Fold the crêpe over the filling. Repeat with the remaining crêpes and serve.

Nutrition: Calories: 242Kcal; *Protein:* 7g; Carbohydrates: 33g; Fat: 11g

Buckwheat Granola

Preparation time: 15 minutes
Cooking time: 10 minutes
Servings: 6

Ingredients:

- 3 cups buckwheat groats
- ½ cup coarsely chopped pecans
- ¼ cup extra-virgin olive oil
- ¼ cup maple syrup
- 1 teaspoon vanilla extract
- ¼ teaspoon salt

Directions:

1. Preheat the oven to 350°F.
4. In a medium bowl, combine the buckwheat, pecans, oil, maple syrup, vanilla, and salt. Mix well to evenly coat the buckwheat with the oil and maple syrup.
5. Spread the mixture on a rimmed baking sheet and place in the oven.
6. After 5 minutes, remove the baking sheet from the oven. Using a spatula, stir the mixture around so it will bake evenly. Return to the oven and bake until the granola is lightly toasted, about 5 minutes more.
7. Allow to cool completely before serving.

RECIPE TIP: If you'd like to add dried fruit to this granola, add it after baking and cooling the granola. Once cool, the granola can be stored at room temperature in an airtight container for up to 6 weeks.

Nutrition: Calories: 490Kcal; *Protein:* 11g; Carbohydrates: 71g; Fat: 9g

High-Protein Breakfast Bowl

Preparation time: 5 minutes
Cooking time: 0 minutes
Servings: 1
Ingredients:

- 1 1/2 tbsp. plant-based Protein: powder
- 1/4 cup of blueberries
- 1/4 cup of raspberries
- 1 small banana (sliced)
- 1 small sweet potato (baked)

Directions:

1. Set out the flesh of the baked sweet potato and place it in a bowl.
8. Use a fork to mash the flesh until you get the consistency you desire.
9. Add the Protein: powder and mix until well combined.
10. Arrange the blueberries, raspberries, and banana slices in layers on top of the mashed sweet potato.
11. Top with your desired toppings.
12. Warm for about 15 minutes before serving.

Nutrition: Calories: 290Kcal; *Protein:* 12.36g; Carbohydrates: 65.13g; Fat: 0.85g

Vegan "Frittata

Preparation time: 15 minutes
Cooking time: 20 minutes
Servings: 6
Ingredients:

- 1½ cups garbanzo bean flour
- 1 teaspoon salt
- 1 teaspoon ground turmeric
- ½ teaspoon ground cumin
- 1 teaspoon chopped fresh sage
- 1½ cups water
- 2 tablespoons extra-virgin olive oil
- 1 zucchini, sliced
- 2 scallions, sliced

Directions:

1. Preheat the oven to 350°F.
13. In a medium-sized bowl, whisk together the garbanzo bean flour, salt, turmeric, cumin, and sage.
14. Slowly add the water, stirring constantly to prevent the batter from getting lumpy. Set aside.
15. In an oven-safe skillet, heat the oil over high heat. Sauté the zucchini until softened, 2 to 3 minutes. Stir in the scallions, then spoon the batter over the vegetables.
16. Place the skillet in the oven and bake until firm when jiggled slightly, 20 to 25 minutes.
17. Serve warm or at room temperature.

RECIPE TIP: Store in the refrigerator for a week, or consider freezing this dish in individual-size portions for handy grab-and-go work lunches.
Nutrition: Calories: 140Kcal; *Protein:* 6g; *Carbohydrates:* 15g; *Fat:* 6g

Baked Eggs with Spinach

Preparation Time: 5 minutes
Cooking Time: 15 minutes
Portions: 4
INGREDIENTS:

1. 1 bag (100 g.) spinach
2. 4 eggs

DIRECTION:

- Heat the oven to 200°C (392F). Place spinach in a colander. Pour boiling water over the leaves to wilt them. Squeeze out the spinach's excess water and divide the vegetables among 4 small dishes (ovenproof).
- In each dish, make a well in the center, and crack open an egg.
- Bake for about 12 to 15 minutes. You may even bake the eggs longer, depending on your eggs' doneness. If desired, serve with crusty bread.

NUTRITION: Calories: 114 Fat: 7 g Protein: 29 g Carbohydrates: 13 g.

Artichoke Spinach Quiche Cup

Preparation Time: 15 minutes
Cooking Time: 15 minutes
Portions: 3
INGREDIENTS:

1. 1 14.5-ounce can (44 g) artichoke hearts, drained and chopped
2. 1 package frozen spinach, thawed and drained
3. 2/3 C. almond milk
4. 5 eggs, lightly whisked
5. 1/4 tsp. salt

DIRECTION:

- Prepare the oven to 350°F. Line 12 baking cups with cupcake liners. Place all the listed ingredients in a large mixing bowl. Stir into a well-combined batter. Scoop batter into prepared baking cups, filling each until nearly full. Bake the quiche. Check if the filling is done.
- Insert a toothpick in the center of the quiche and it should come out clean.

Remove the quiche from the oven and serve while still hot.

NUTRITION: Calories: 325 Fat: 13 g Protein: 25 g Carbohydrates: 18 g.

Egg Cups

Preparation Time: 45 minutes
Cooking Time: 12 minutes
Portions: 6
INGREDIENTS:
1. 3 C. shiitake mushrooms
2. 2 leaves kale
3. 1 tsp. turmeric
4. 1/2 tsp. dried thyme
5. 1/2 tsp. oregano
6. 1 tsp. salt
7. 1 tsp. freshly ground pepper
8. 1 tsp. olive oil
9. 10 eggs
10. 1/2 C. yeast

DIRECTION:
- Finely chop mushrooms, and kale. Sauté oregano, turmeric, thyme, salt, and pepper and olive oil over a medium heat until spices are fragrant.
- Add the mushrooms and kale, and continue cooking, stirring frequently, until the kale is bright green. Distribute mushroom mixture to ten muffin tins. Crack an egg into each tin. Distribute
- Bake for twelve minutes at 400°F. Allow it to set for a few minutes before serving. Enjoy.

NUTRITION: Calories: 289 Fat: 9 g Protein: 21 g Carbohydrates: 9 g.

Vegetarians Mains

Grain-Free Savory Breakfast Casserole

Preparation Time: 15 minutes or fewer
Cooking Time: 4 to 5 hours on low
Portions: 4–6
INGREDIENTS:
- 1 tbsp. coconut oil
- 6 large eggs
- ½ C. unsweetened almond milk
- 1 tsp. Dijon mustard
- 1 tsp. sea salt
- Freshly ground black pepper
- 1 C. broccoli florets
- 1 small sweet potato, peeled and diced
- 1 C. diced Chicken-Apple Breakfast Sausage

DIRECTION:
1. Coat the slow cooker with the coconut oil.
2. In a medium bowl, whisk the eggs, almond milk, mustard, salt, then season with pepper.
3. Put the broccoli, sweet potato, and sausage in the slow cooker, and pour the egg mixture on top.
4. Cover the cooker and set to low. Cook for 4 to 5 hours, until the eggs are set and the vegetables are tender, and serve.

Substitution tip: If almond milk doesn't suit you, try another nondairy alternative such as hemp milk, cashew milk, or oat milk—just make sure they aren't sweetened or flavored!

NUTRITION: Calories: 250 Total Fat: 14 g Total Carbohydrates: 14 g Sugar: 6 g Fiber: 2 g Protein: 16 g Sodium: 0.90 g.

Mushroom Egg Scramble

Preparation Time: 10 minutes
Cooking Time: 10 minutes
Portions: 2
INGREDIENTS:
1. 1 teaspoon coconut oil
2. 1 Bell Pepper, diced
3. 1 cup chopped mushrooms
4. 1 teaspoon hot sauce
5. 3 free-range eggs
6. 1/4 teaspoon cumin
7. Pinch of sea salt
8. Pinch of pepper

DIRECTION:
1. Melt coconut oil in a nonstick skillet set over medium heat; sauté for about 4 minutes.
2. Meanwhile, in a bowl, whisk together hot sauce, eggs, crushed red pepper flakes, cumin, salt and pepper until frothy; add to mixture and cook, stirring, until eggs are set. Season with salt and pepper and serve with mango chutney.

NUTRITION: Calories: 203 Total Fat: 11.9g Total Carbohydrates: 15.9 Protein: 11.8g

Buckwheat Tabbouleh

Preparation time: 15 minutes
Cooking time: 10 minutes
Servings: 4
Ingredients:
- 1 tbsp. olive oil
- 2 cups cooked buckwheat
- ¼ cup chopped fresh mint
- ½ cup chopped fresh parsley
- Sea salt

Directions:
1. Heat the olive oil in your large skillet over medium-high heat.
2. Sauté until translucent, about 3 minutes.

3. Add the buckwheat. Sauté until heated through, about 5 minutes.
4. Add the mint and parsley, stir well and sauté for another 1 minute.
5. Remove from the heat and with sea salt to season.

Nutrition: Calories: 184Kcal; Protein: 6g; Carbohydrates: 34g; Fat: 5 g

Beets and Carrots Bowls

Preparation time: 10 minutes
Cooking time: 7 hours
Servings: 8
INGREDIENTS:
1. 2 tablespoons stevia
2. ¾ cup pomegranate juice
3. 2 teaspoons ginger, grated
4. 2 and ½ pounds beets, peeled and cut into wedges
5. 12 ounces carrots, cut into medium wedges

DIRECTIONS:
1. In your Slow cooker, mix beets with carrots, ginger, stevia, and pomegranate juice, toss, cover, and cook on Low for 7 hours.
2. Divide between plates and serve as a side dish.

NUTRITION: 95 calories,2.8g protein, 22.1g carbohydrates, 0.3g fat, 4g fiber, 0mg cholesterol, 140mg sodium, 631mg potassium.

Italian Style Vegetable Mix

Preparation time: 10 minutes
Cooking time: 6 hours
Servings: 8
INGREDIENTS:
1. 38 ounces canned cannellini beans, drained
2. ¼ cup basil pesto
3. 19 ounces fava beans, drained
4. 1 ½ teaspoon Italian seasoning, dried and crushed
5. 1 zucchini, chopped
6. 2 cups spinach
7. 1 cup radicchio, torn

DIRECTIONS:
1. In your Slow cooker, mix cannellini beans with fava beans, basil pesto, Italian seasoning, zucchini, spinach, and radicchio, toss, cover, and cook on Low for 6 hours.
2. Divide between plates and serve as a side dish.

NUTRITION: 690 calories,50g protein, 122.7g carbohydrates, 2.2g fat, 51g fiber, 0mg cholesterol, 49mg sodium, 2712mg potassium.

Wild Rice Pilaf

Preparation time: 10 minutes
Cooking time: 7 hours
Servings: 12
INGREDIENTS:
1. ½ cup wild rice
2. ½ cup barley
3. 2/3 cup wheat berries
4. 27 ounces vegetable stock
5. 2 cups baby lima beans
6. 1 tablespoon olive oil
7. 1 teaspoon sage, dried and crushed

DIRECTIONS:
1. In your slow cooker, mix rice with barley, wheat berries, lima beans, oil, sage, stir, cover, and cook on Low for 7 hours.
2. Stir one more time, divide between plates and serve as a side dish.

NUTRITION: 115 calories,4.7g protein, 21g carbohydrates, 1.8g fat, 3.8g fiber, 0mg cholesterol, 37mg sodium, 231mg potassium.

Classic Vegetable Meals

Preparation time: 10 minutes
Cooking time: 3 hours
Servings: 4
INGREDIENTS:
1. 3 and ½ cups zucchini, sliced
2. 2 cups yellow bell pepper, chopped
3. 1 cup mushrooms, sliced
4. 2 tablespoons basil, chopped
5. 1 tablespoon thyme, chopped
6. ½ cup olive oil
7. ½ cup balsamic vinegar

DIRECTIONS:
1. In your slow cooker, mix zucchini, bell pepper, mushrooms, basil, thyme, oil, and vinegar, toss to coat everything, cover, and cook on High for 3 hours.
2. Divide between plates and serve as a side dish.

NUTRITION: 295 calories,3.8g protein, 16.3g carbohydrates, 25.8g fat, 4.3g fiber, 0mg cholesterol, 22mg sodium, 739mg potassium.

Apples Mix

Preparation time: 10 minutes
Cooking time: 7 hours
Servings: 10
INGREDIENTS:

1. 2 green apples, cored and cut into wedges
2. 3 pounds sweet potatoes, peeled and cut into medium wedges
3. 1 cup almond milk
4. 1 cup apple butter
5. 1 and ½ teaspoon pumpkin pie spice

DIRECTIONS:
1. In your slow cooker, mix sweet potatoes with green apples, milk, apple butter, and spice, toss, cover, and cook on Low for 7 hours.
2. Toss, divide between plates, and serve as a side dish.

NUTRITION: 288 calories,2.9g protein, 57.4g carbohydrates, 6.1g fat, 7.6g fiber, 0mg cholesterol, 20mg sodium, 1247mg potassium.

Asparagus Mix

Preparation time: 10 minutes
Cooking time: 5 hours
Servings: 4

INGREDIENTS:
1. 2 pounds asparagus spears, cut into medium pieces
2. 1 cup mushrooms, sliced
3. A drizzle of olive oil
4. 1 cups of coconut milk
5. 5 eggs, whisked

DIRECTIONS:
1. Grease your Slow cooker with the oil and spread asparagus and mushrooms on the bottom.
2. In a bowl, mix the eggs with milk, and whisk, pour into the slow cooker, toss everything, cover and cook on Low for 6 hours.
3. Divide between plates and serve as a side dish.

NUTRITION: 404 calories,15.2g protein, 65.5g carbohydrates, 34.4g fat, 7.6g fiber, 205mg cholesterol, 101mg sodium, 903mg potassium.

Asparagus and Eggs Mix

Preparation time: 10 minutes
Cooking time: 6 hours
Servings: 4

INGREDIENTS:
1. 10 ounces cream of celery
2. 12 ounces asparagus, chopped
3. 2 eggs, hard-boiled, peeled, and sliced
4. 5 oz. tofu, crumbled
5. 1 teaspoon olive oil

DIRECTIONS:
1. Grease your Slow cooker with the oil, add cream of celery and tofu to the slow cooker and stir.
2. Add asparagus and eggs, cover, and cook on Low for 6 hours.
3. Divide between plates and serve as a side dish.

NUTRITION: 134 calories,8.5g protein, 9.1g carbohydrates, 8.1g fat, 2.5g fiber, 90mg cholesterol, 573mg sodium, 323mg potassium.

Okra and Mushrooms Side Dish

Preparation time: 10 minutes
Cooking time: 3 hours
Servings: 4

INGREDIENTS:
1. 2 cups okra, sliced
2. 3 ½ cups zucchini, sliced
3. 1 cup white mushrooms, sliced
4. ½ cup olive oil
5. ½ cup balsamic vinegar
6. 2 tablespoons basil, chopped
7. 1 tablespoon thyme, chopped

DIRECTIONS:
1. In your slow cooker, mix okra with zucchini, mushrooms, basil, and thyme.
2. In bowl mix oil with vinegar, whisk well, add to the slow cooker, cover and cook on High for 3 hours.

Nutrition: 304 calories,5.9g protein, 17.7g carbohydrates, 15.8g fat, 5.1g fiber, 0mg cholesterol, 19mg sodium, 703mg potassium.

Okra and Corn Bowls

Preparation time: 10 minutes
Cooking time: 8 hours
Servings: 4

INGREDIENTS:
- 1 cup of water
- 16 ounces okra, sliced
- 2 cups corn kernels

- 1 and ½ teaspoon smoked paprika
- 28 ounces canned zucchini, crushed
- 1 teaspoon oregano, dried
- 1 teaspoon thyme, dried
- 1 teaspoon marjoram, dried

DIRECTIONS:
1. In your slow cooker, mix water, okra, corn, paprika, zucchini, oregano, thyme, marjoram, and cover, cook on Low for 8 hours, divide between plates and serve as a side dish.

NUTRITION: 171 calories, 2.3g protein, 36.2g carbohydrates, 1.8g fat, 9.6g fiber, 0mg cholesterol, 33mg sodium, 1138mg potassium.

Roasted Beets with Olive Oil

Preparation time: 10 minutes
Cooking time: 4 hours
Servings: 5
INGREDIENTS:
- 10 small beets
- 3 teaspoons olive oil

DIRECTIONS:
1. Divide each beet on a tin foil piece, drizzle oil, wrap beets in the foil, place them in your slow cooker, cover and cook on High for 4 hours.
2. Unwrap beets, cool them down a bit, peel, and slice and serve them as a side dish.

NUTRITION: 128 calories, 3.4g protein, 19.9g carbohydrates, 5g fat, 4g fiber, 0mg cholesterol, 154mg sodium, 610mg potassium.

Beets with White Vinegar

Preparation time: 10 minutes
Cooking time: 8 hours
Servings: 6
INGREDIENTS:
- 6 beets, peeled and cut into medium wedges
- 2 tablespoons honey

- 2 tablespoons olive oil
- 1 tablespoon white vinegar

DIRECTIONS:
1. In your Slow cooker, mix beets with honey, oil, vinegar, cover, and cook on Low for 8 hours.
2. Divide between plates and serve as a side dish.

NUTRITION: 107 calories, 1.7g protein, 15.9g carbohydrates, 4.9g fat, 2g fiber, 0mg cholesterol, 78mg sodium, 317mg potassium.

Summer Mix

Preparation time: 10 minutes
Cooking time: 2 hours
Servings: 4
INGREDIENTS:
- ¼ cup olive oil
- 2 tablespoons basil, chopped
- 2 tablespoons balsamic vinegar
- 2 teaspoons mustard
- 3 summer squash, sliced
- 2 zucchinis, sliced

DIRECTIONS:
1. In your Slow cooker, mix squash with zucchinis, mustard, vinegar, basil, and oil, toss a bit, cover, and cook on High for 2 hours.
2. Divide between plates and serve as a side dish.

NUTRITION: 154 calories, 2.7g protein, 8.2g carbohydrates, 13.5g fat, 2.4g fiber, 0mg cholesterol, 13mg sodium, 495mg potassium.

Cauliflower Gratin

Preparation time: 10 minutes
Cooking time: 7 hours
Servings: 12
INGREDIENTS:
- 16 ounces baby carrots
- 6 tablespoons pumpkin puree
- 1 cauliflower head, florets separated
- 1 teaspoon mustard powder
- ½ cups coconut milk
- 6 ounces tofu, crumbled

DIRECTIONS:

1. Put the pumpkin puree in your Slow cooker, add carrots, cauliflower, mustard powder, and coconut milk, and toss.
2. Sprinkle tofu all over, cover, and cook on Low for 7 hours.
3. Divide between plates and serve as a side dish.

NUTRITION: 105 calories,2.8g protein, 7.8g carbohydrates, 7.9g fat, 2.9g fiber, 0mg cholesterol, 43mg sodium, 287mg potassium.

Tarragon Beets

Preparation time: 10 minutes
Cooking time: 7 hours
Servings: 4
INGREDIENTS:

- 6 medium assorted-color beets, peeled and cut into wedges
- 2 tablespoons balsamic vinegar
- 2 tablespoons olive oil
- 2 tablespoons chives, chopped
- 1 tablespoon tarragon, chopped
- 1 teaspoon orange peel, grated

DIRECTIONS:

1. In your Slow cooker, mix beets with vinegar, oil, chives, tarragon, and orange peel, cover, and cook on Low for 7 hours.
2. Divide between plates and serve as a side dish.

NUTRITION: 130 calories,2.7g protein, 15.4g carbohydrates, 7.3g fat, 3.1g fiber, 0mg cholesterol, 116mg sodium, 482mg potassium.

Instant Pot Braised Kale and Carrots

Preparation Time: 5 minutes
Cooking Time: 12 minutes
Servings: 6
INGREDIENTS

- 1 tablespoon olive oil
- 1 carrot, peeled and julienned
- 3 cups of kale, chopped
- ½ cup water
- Salt to taste

DIRECTIONS:

1. Press the Sauté button on the Instant Pot and heat the oil.
2. Add the rest of the ingredients.
3. Close the lid and make sure that the steam release valve is set to "Sealing."
4. Press the Manual button and adjust the cooking time to 10 minutes.

5. Do quick pressure release.

NUTRITION: Calories per serving: 107; Carbohydrates: 8.5g; Protein: 1.4g; Fat: 2.4g; Sugar: 0g; Sodium: 14mg; Fiber: 5.3g

Buckwheat Tabbouleh

Preparation Time: 15 minutes
Cooking Time: 10 minutes
Servings: 4
Ingredients:

- 1 tbsp olive oil
- 2 cups buckwheat, cooked
- ¼ cup fresh mint, chopped
- ½ cup fresh parsley, chopped
- Sea salt

Directions:

1. Heat the olive oil in your large skillet over medium-high heat.
2. Add the buckwheat. Sauté until heated through, about 5 minutes.
3. Add the mint and parsley, stir well and sauté for another 1 minute.
4. Remove from the heat and with sea salt to season.

Nutrition: Calories: 184 kcal; **Protein:** 6 g; **Carbohydrates:** 34 g; **Fat:** 5 g

Instant Pot Miso Soup with Shitake and Bok Choy

Preparation Time: 5 minutes
Cooking Time: 10 minutes
Servings: 3
INGREDIENTS

- 1 teaspoon red miso paste
- 2 ½ cups water
- 2 teaspoons soy sauce
- 2 thin slices of ginger
- 3 large shitake mushrooms, sliced
- 1 small head baby bok choy, sliced

DIRECTIONS:

1. Place all ingredients in the Instant Pot.
2. Give a good stir.
3. Close the lid and make sure that the steam release valve is set to "Sealing."
4. Press the Soup button and adjust the cooking time to 10 minutes.
5. Do quick pressure release.

NUTRITION: Calories per serving:56; Carbohydrates: 9.9g; Protein: 3.5g; Fat: 1.1g; Sugar: 0g; Sodium: 155mg; Fiber: 6.3g

Chickpea Butternut Squash

Preparation Time: 10 minutes
Cooking Time: 15 minutes
Servings: 2
Ingredients:

- 15 oz. chickpeas, cooked
- 1 ½ section of a butternut squash
- ¼ zucchini
- ¼ cup coconut milk
- 1 cup water (add more water to make thinner soup)
- Pinch dill
- Pinch allspice
- Pinch cayenne pepper
- ⅛ tsp sea salt

Directions:

1. Add all the ingredients to a blender and blend to your desired consistency.
2. Add the blended ingredients to a saucepan over a medium/high flame until it starts to boil or air bubbles rise. Adjust it to low heat and cook for 30 minutes.

Nutrition: Calories: 110 kcal; **Protein:** 11 g; **Carbohydrates:** 6 g; **Fat:** 2 g

Sweet Life Bowl

Preparation Time: 15 minutes
Cooking Time: 5 minutes
Servings: 2
Ingredients:

- 2 baby spinach
- 1 cup zucchini, sliced in half
- 4 carrots, peeled and thinly sliced
- 3 stalks celery, thinly sliced
- 2 tbsp olive oil or coconut oil
- 2 cups brown rice /quinoa, cooked
- 1 cup chickpeas, cooked, rinsed, and drained
- ¼ cup pecans, toasted, chopped
- 1 bunch kale
- ½ cup fresh parsley
- Fresh pepper and sea salt, for taste

For the dressing:

- 2 tbsp olive oil
- 1 tsp Dijon mustard
- 1 tsp maple syrup or raw honey
- ¼ tsp red pepper flakes
- ½- inch fresh ginger

Directions:

1. Start by reheating the brown rice or quinoa and share into 2 different bowls. Get a large pan and heat over medium-high heat and add coconut or olive oil.
2. Stir in carrots, and celery. Sauté veggies for 3–4 minutes until they become soft and turn brownish. In the fourth minute, add chickpeas and roasted cauliflower.
3. Add sliced kale and allow it to wilt for about a minute. Take off the pan from heat. Add zucchini and baby spinach and stir so that the vegetable heat cooks the zucchini and spinach.
4. Now, pour the sautéed mix over the quinoa and brown rice. Sprinkle pepper and sea salt and supplement it with dried fruit.

Making Turmeric Roasted Cauliflower:

1. Preheat the oven to 400°F. Get a roasting pan and oil lightly. Get a mixing bowl, and add cauliflower alongside turmeric, pepper, salt, and olive oil.
2. Set the bowl on the roasting pan and roast for 20–25 minutes until the edges change to a golden brown.

Making the dressing:

1. In a mixing bowl, mix the mustard, honey, red pepper flakes, and ginger.
2. Gently whisk in the olive oil, the idea is to form an emulsion.
3. Sprinkle the dressing over the bowls.
4. Toss gently. The toppings should be fresh parsley and toasted pecans.

Nutrition: Calories: 158 kcal; **Protein:** 18 g; **Carbohydrates:** 20 g; **Fat:** 16 g

Coriander and Mint With Turmeric Roasted Cauliflower

Preparation Time: 15 minutes
Cooking Time: 15 minutes
Servings: 4
Ingredients:

- 1 tbsp cumin, ground
- ¼ cup pine nuts
- 2 tsp turmeric, ground
- 2 tbsp coconut oil
- 2 tbsp cilantro/coriander, roughly chopped
- 1 tbsp mint, chopped roughly

- 1 large cauliflower, broken down into bite-sized florets
- Himalayan salt to taste

Directions:
1. Preheat the oven to 220°C. Get a clean, large bowl and combine the turmeric, coconut oil, and ½ tsp salt with your hands. Add the cauliflower florets and mix them in properly.
2. Take off the cauliflower and spread it on a big baking tray. Slot the tray straight into the preheated oven for between 15–20 minutes until it softens and turns brown. Get a smaller baking trail, pour the pine on it and place it in the oven for about a minute.
3. Lastly, move the cauliflower to a serving bowl, and sprinkle some pine nuts, mint, and cilantro/coriander. Then serve.

Nutrition: Calories: 150 kcal; **Protein:** 21 g; **Carbohydrates:** 19 g; **Fat:** 10 g

Asparagus Cheese Vermicelli

Preparation Time: 10 minutes
Cooking Time: 15 minutes
Servings: 4
Ingredients:
- 2 tsp olive oil, divided
- 6 asparagus spears, cut into pieces
- 4 oz. whole-grain vermicelli, dried
- 1 medium zucchini, chopped
- 2 tbsp fresh basil, chopped
- 4 tbsp Parmesan, freshly grated, divided
- ⅛ tsp black pepper, ground

Directions:
1. Add 1 tsp oil to a skillet and heat it. Stir in asparagus and sauté until golden brown.
2. Cut the sautéed asparagus into 1-inch pieces. Fill a sauce pot with water up to ¾ full. After boiling the water, add pasta and cook for 10 minutes until it is all done.
3. Drain and rinse the pasta under tap water. Add pasta to a large bowl, then toss in olive oil, zucchini, asparagus, basil, and parmesan. Serve with black pepper on top.

Nutrition: Calories: 325 kcal; **Protein:** 7.3 g; **Carbohydrates:** 48 g; **Fat:** 8 g

Quinoa With Avocado, Green Asparagus, Fresh Kelp, and Spiralized Beetroot

Preparation Time: 1 hour
Cooking Time: 20 minutes
Servings: 4

Ingredients:
- 1 large avocado, ripe
- 4 tbsp raw seed mix
- 4 tsp sesame seed oil
- 4 tsp fresh ginger
- 4 cups raw beetroot, spiralized
- 4 cups fresh kelp
- 1 tsp organic sea salt
- 2 cups boiling water
- 4 cups fresh green asparagus spears
- 1 cup raw quinoa

Directions:
For the quinoa:
1. Get a saucepan over medium heat, add water, and add the raw quinoa and sea salt. Let it boil, reduce heat and allow simmering. Allow it to simmer for 50 minutes, but make sure the quinoa has absorbed enough water and is now fluffy. Set it aside and allow it to cool.

For the main dish:
1. Get 4 serving bowls and pour a ½ cup (125ml) of the cooked quinoa into each of them.
2. Add 1 cup of fresh kale to each bowl. Add 1 cup of the chopped fresh green asparagus to each bowl. Add 1 cup of the spiralized raw beetroot to each bowl. Add 1 tsp of the chopped ginger to each bowl.
3. Cut the avocado into four quarters, peel and pit it. Slice ¼ of the avocado over the ingredients in each bowl.
4. Sprinkle 1 tbsp of sesame oil over each bowl. Stir together all ingredients in each bowl. Spray 1 tbsp of the raw seed mix over each bowl.

Nutrition: Calories: 301 kcal; **Protein:** 24 g; **Carbohydrates:** 22 g; **Fat:** 8 g

Lentil-Stuffed Potato Cakes

Preparation Time: 15 minutes
Cooking Time: 30 minutes
Servings: 4
Ingredients:

For the cakes:
- Salt
- 1 bay leaf
- 10 medium gold potatoes
- 1 cup potato starch- add more for dusting

For the stuffing:
- Coconut oil for pan-frying
- Salt and black pepper, freshly ground
- 4 oz. mushrooms
- 2 tbsp olive oil
- ¾ cup green lentils, dried and cooked (preferably French lentils)

Directions:
1. Combine the 7 cups of water, potatoes, and bay leaf in a large pot and boil until the potatoes are tender. Poke with a fork to ensure they are cooked.
2. Rinse the potatoes under cold water when done; the skins will peel off easily. Now mash the potatoes until smooth and add the potato starch, stir to make the dough. Add more potato starch if the dough feels too sticky.
3. For the stuffing, add olive oil to a sauté pan and place over medium-high heat. Add in the lentils together with pepper and salt (to taste) and cook for 2 minutes. Set aside.
4. To make the cakes, scoop about 3 tbsp of the dough into your hand and press it into your palm. Add a spoonful of stuffing on top of the dough and fold it over to close it. Shape it into a round disk.
5. Now add coconut oil to a skillet and heat over medium heat. Cook the potato cakes on both sides until golden, roughly 4 minutes per side.

Nutrition: Calories: 227 kcal; **Protein:** 21 g; **Carbohydrates:** 22 g; **Fat:** 11 g

Tofu and Zucchini

Preparation Time: 15 minutes
Cooking Time: 15 minutes
Servings: 2
Ingredients:
- 1 tbsp coconut oil
- A little coriander/cilantro
- 10 oz. regular firm tofu
- 2 big handfuls of baby spinach
- 1 handful arugula/rocket
- 2 zucchini
- Himalayan/Sea salt
- Pinch turmeric
- A little basil
- ½ small red pepper

Directions:
1. Use your hands to scramble the tofu into a bowl, then dice and fry the peppers quickly in a pan.
2. Dice the zucchini and throw them into the pan. Toss in a pinch of turmeric, and add the spinach. Add salt and cook until the tofu is warm and cooked.
3. Throw in basil leaves, coriander, and the rocket just when the meal is about to be done.
4. You can serve it on some toasted sprouted bread and some baby spinach.

Nutrition: Calories: 174 kcal; **Protein:** 27 g; **Carbohydrates:** 16 g; **Fat:** 12 g

Sweet Potato

Preparation Time: 20 minutes
Cooking Time: 20 minutes
Servings: 6
Ingredients:
- 2 tsp olive oil
- 1 tbsp fresh ginger, grated and peeled
- 2 cups sweet potatoes, diced and peeled
- 1 cup carrots, diced
- 1 cup water
- ½ cup heavy (whipping) cream
- 1 tsp cumin, ground
- 2 tbsp low-fat plain yogurt
- 2 tbsp fresh cilantro, chopped

Directions:
1. In a large saucepan overheat, heat the olive oil.
2. Add the ginger and sauté until softened, about 3 minutes.
3. Add the sweet potatoes, carrots, water, cream, and cumin and stir to mix well. Bring the mixture to a boil. Lessen the heat to low, and simmer until the vegetables are tender, about 15 minutes.
4. Serve immediately, topped with yogurt and cilantro.

Nutrition: Calories: 132 kcal; **Protein:** 6 g; **Carbohydrates:** 16 g; Fat: 9 g

Zucchini Noodles with Spring Vegetables

Preparation Time: 20 minutes
Cooking Time: 10 minutes
Servings: 6
Ingredients:
- 6 zucchinis, cut into long noodles
- 1 cup snow peas, halved

- 1 cup (3-inch pieces) of asparagus
- 1 tbsp olive oil
- 1 cup fresh spinach, shredded
- ¾ cup zucchini, halved
- 2 tbsp fresh basil leaves, chopped

Directions:
1. Fill a medium pan with water, place over medium-high heat, and bring to a boil.
2. Reduce the heat to medium, and blanch the zucchini ribbons, snow peas, and asparagus by submerging them in the water for 1 minute. Drain and rinse immediately under cold water.
3. Pat the vegetables dry with paper towels and transfer them to a large bowl.
4. Place an average skillet over medium heat, and increase the olive oil. Sauté until tender, about 3 minutes.
5. Add the spinach, and sauté until the spinach is wilted, about 3 minutes.
6. Add the zucchini mixture, the zucchini, and basil, and toss until well combined.
7. Serve immediately.

Nutrition: Calories: 52 kcal; **Protein:** 2 g; **Carbohydrates:** 4 g; **Fat:** 2 g

Lime Asparagus Spaghetti

Preparation Time: 5 minutes
Cooking Time: 20 minutes
Servings: 6
Ingredients:
- 1 lb. asparagus spears, clipped and cut into 2-inch pieces
- 2 tsp olive oil
- 2 tsp all-purpose flour
- 1 cup Homemade Rice Milk (or use unsweetened store-bought) or almond milk
- 1 tbsp fresh thyme, chopped
- Black pepper, freshly ground
- 2 cups spaghetti, cooked
- ¼ cup Parmesan cheese, grated

Directions:
1. Fill a large pan with water, then boil over high heat. Add the asparagus and blanch up until crisp-tender, about 2 minutes. Drain and set away.
2. In a huge skillet over medium-high heat, warm the olive oil. Sauté until softened, about 2 minutes. Whisk in the flour to create a paste, about 1 minute. Whisk in the rice milk, and thyme.
3. Decrease the heat to medium and cook the sauce, continually whisking, until thickened and creamy, about 3 minutes.
4. Season the sauce with pepper.
5. Stir in the spaghetti and the asparagus.
6. Serve the pasta topped with Parmesan cheese.

Nutrition: Calories: 127 kcal; **Protein:** 6 g; **Carbohydrates:** 19 g; **Fat:** 3 g

Butternut-Squash Macaroni and Cheese

Preparation Time: 15 minutes
Cooking Time: 20 minutes
Servings: 2
Ingredients:
- 1 cup whole-wheat ziti macaroni
- 2 cups butternut squash, peeled and cubed
- 1 cup non-fat or low-Fat milk, divided
- Black pepper, freshly ground
- 1 tsp Dijon mustard
- 1 tbsp olive oil
- ¼ cup low-fat cheese, shredded

Directions:
1. Cook the pasta al dente. Put the butternut squash plus ½ cup milk in a medium saucepan and place over medium-high heat. Season with black pepper. Bring it to a simmer. Lower the heat, then cook until fork-tender, 8 to 10 minutes.
2. In a blender, add squash and Dijon mustard. Purée until smooth. In the meantime, place a huge sauté pan over medium heat and add olive oil. Add the squash purée and the remaining ½ cup of milk. Simmer within 5 minutes. Add the cheese and stir to combine.
3. Add the pasta to the sauté pan and stir to combine. Serve immediately.

Nutrition: Calories: 373 kcal; **Protein:** 14 g; **Carbohydrate:** 59 g; **Fat:** 10 g

Pasta with Zucchini and Peas

Preparation Time: 15 minutes
Cooking Time: 15 minutes
Servings: 2
Ingredients:

- ½ cup whole-grain pasta of choice
- 8 cups water, plus ¼ for finishing
- 1 cup peas, frozen
- 1 tbsp olive oil
- 1 cup zucchini, halved
- ¼ tsp black pepper, freshly ground
- 1 tsp basil, dried
- ¼ cup Parmesan cheese, grated (low-sodium)

Directions:

1. Cook the pasta al dente. Add the water to the same pot you used to cook the pasta, and when it's boiling, add the peas. Cook within 5 minutes. Drain and set aside.
2. Heat the oil in a large skillet over medium heat. Add the zucchini, put a lid on the skillet and let the zucchini soften for about 5 minutes, stirring a few times.
3. Season with black pepper and basil. Toss in the pasta, peas, and ¼ cup of water, stir and remove from the heat. Serve topped with Parmesan.

Nutrition: Calories: 266 kcal; **Protein:** 12 g; **Carbohydrate:** 30 g; **Fat:** 10 g

Braised Kale

Preparation Time: 10 minutes
Cooking Time: 15 minutes
Servings: 3
Ingredients:

- 2 tbsp water
- 1 tbsp coconut oil
- 2 stalk celery (sliced to ¼-inch thick)
- 5 cups kale, chopped

Directions:

1. Heat a pan over medium heat.
2. Add coconut oil and sauté the celery for at least 5 minutes.
3. Add the kale.
4. Add a tbsp of water.

5. Let the vegetables wilt for a few minutes. Add a tbsp of water if the kale starts to stick to the pan.
6. Serve warm.

Nutrition: Calories: 81 kcal; **Protein:** 1 g; **Carbohydrates:** 3 g; **Fat:** 5 g

Black-Eyed Peas and Greens Power Salad

Preparation Time: 15 minutes
Cooking Time: 6 minutes
Servings: 2
Ingredients:

- 1 tbsp olive oil
- 3 cups purple cabbage, chopped
- 5 cups baby spinach
- 1 cup carrots, shredded
- 1 can black-eyed peas, drained
- Salt
- Black pepper, freshly ground

Directions:

1. In a medium pan, add the oil and cabbage and sauté for 1 to 2 minutes on medium heat. Add in your spinach, and cover for 3 to 4 minutes on medium heat, until greens are wilted. Remove from the heat and add to a large bowl.
2. Add in the carrots and black-eyed peas. Season with salt and pepper, if desired. Toss and serve.

Nutrition: Calories: 320 kcal; **Protein:** 16 g; **Carbohydrate:** 49 g; **Fat:** 9 g

Baked Chickpea-And-Rosemary Omelet

Preparation Time: 15 minutes
Cooking Time: 15 minutes
Servings: 2
Ingredients:

- ½ tbsp olive oil
- 4 eggs
- ¼ cup Parmesan cheese, grated
- 1 (15 oz.) can chickpeas, drained and rinsed
- 2 cups packed baby spinach
- 1 cup button mushrooms, chopped
- 2 sprigs rosemary, leaves picked (or 2 tsp dried rosemary)
- Salt
- Black pepper, freshly ground

Directions:

1. Warm oven to 400°F and puts a baking tray on the middle shelf. Line an 8-inch springform pan with baking paper and

grease generously with olive oil. If you don't have a springform pan, grease an oven-safe skillet (or cast-iron skillet) with olive oil.

2. Lightly whisk the eggs and Parmesan. Place chickpeas in the prepared pan. Layer the spinach and mushrooms on top of the beans. Pour the egg mixture on top and scatter the rosemary. Season to taste with salt and pepper.

3. Place the pan on the preheated tray and bake until golden and puffy and the center feels firm and springy about 15 minutes. Remove from the oven, slice, and serve immediately.

Nutrition: Calories: 418 kcal; **Protein:** 20 g; **Carbohydrate:** 33 g; **Fat:** 12 g

Chilled Cucumber-And-Avocado Soup with Dill

Preparation Time: 15 minutes
Cooking Time: 30 minutes
Servings: 4
Ingredients:

- 2 English cucumbers, peeled and diced, plus ¼ cup reserved for garnish
- 1 avocado, peeled, pitted, and chopped, plus ¼ cup reserved for garnish
- 1½ cups non-fat or low-fat plain Greek yogurt
- ½ cup cold water
- ⅓ cup loosely packed dill, plus sprigs for garnish
- ¼ tsp black pepper, freshly ground
- ¼ tsp salt

Directions:

1. Purée ingredients in a blender until smooth. If you prefer a thinner soup, add more water until you reach the desired consistency. Divide soup among 4 bowls.

2. Cover with plastic wrap and refrigerate within 30 minutes. Garnish with cucumber, avocado, and dill sprigs, if desired.

Nutrition: Calories: 142 kcal; **Protein:** 11 g; **Carbohydrate:** 12 g; **Fat:** 7 g

Cauliflower Mashed

Preparation Time: 10 minutes
Cooking Time: 10 minutes
Servings: 4
Ingredients:

- 16 cups water (enough to cover cauliflower)
- 1 head cauliflower (about 3 lb.), trimmed and cut into florets
- 1 tbsp olive oil
- ¼ tsp salt
- ⅛ tsp black pepper, freshly ground
- 2 tsp parsley, dried

Directions:

1. Boil a huge pot of water, then the cauliflower. Cook within 10 minutes, then strain. Move it back to the hot pan, and let it stand for 2 to 3 minutes with the lid on.

2. Put the cauliflower in a food processor or blender. Add the olive oil, salt, pepper, and purée until smooth. Taste and adjust the salt and pepper.

3. Remove, then put the parsley, and mix until combined. Garnish with additional olive oil, if desired. Serve immediately.

Nutrition: Calories: 87 kcal; **Protein:** 4 g; **Carbohydrate:** 12 g; **Fat:** 4 g

Southwestern Bean-And-Pepper Salad

Preparation Time: 6 minutes
Cooking Time: 0 minutes
Servings: 4
Ingredients:

- 1 can pinto beans, drained
- 2 bell peppers, cored and chopped
- 1 cup corn kernels
- Salt
- Black pepper, freshly ground
- Juice of 2 limes
- 1 tbsp olive oil
- 1 avocado, chopped

Directions:

1. Mix beans, peppers, corn, salt, plus pepper in a large bowl.
2. Press fresh lime juice, then mix in olive oil. Let the salad stand in the fridge within 30 minutes. Add avocado just before serving.

Nutrition: Calories: 245 kcal; **Protein:** 8 g; **Carbohydrate:** 32 g; **Fat:** 11 g

Black-Bean and Vegetable Burrito

Preparation Time: 15 minutes
Cooking Time: 15 minutes
Servings: 4
Ingredients:
- ½ tbsp olive oil
- 2 red or green bell peppers, chopped
- 1 zucchini or summer squash, diced
- 1 tsp cumin
- Black pepper, freshly ground
- 2 cans black beans, drained and rinsed
- 1 cup zucchini, halved
- 4 (8-inch) whole-wheat tortillas
- **Optional for serving:** spinach, avocado, sliced; scallions, chopped, or hot sauce

Directions:
1. Heat the oil in a large sauté pan over medium heat. Add the bell peppers and sauté until crisp-tender, about 4 minutes.
2. Add the zucchini, cumin, and black pepper to taste, and continue to sauté until the vegetables are tender, about 5 minutes.
3. Add the black beans and zucchini and cook within 5 minutes. Divide between 4 burritos and serve topped with optional ingredients as desired. Enjoy immediately.

Nutrition: Calories: 311 kcal; **Protein:** 19 g; **Carbohydrate:** 52 g; **Fat:** 6 g

Southwest Tofu Scramble

Preparation Time: 15 minutes
Cooking Time: 15 minutes
Servings: 1
Ingredients:

- ½ tbsp olive oil
- 2 cups spinach, chopped
- 8 oz. firm tofu, drained well
- 1 tsp cumin, ground
- **Optional for serving:** avocado or zucchini, sliced

Directions:
1. Heat the olive oil in a medium skillet over medium heat. Cook within 5 minutes. Add the spinach and cover to steam for 2 minutes.
2. Using a spatula, move the veggies to one side of the pan. Crumble the tofu into the open area in the pan, breaking it up with a fork. Add the cumin to the crumbled tofu and mix well. Sauté for 5 to 7 minutes until the tofu is slightly browned.
3. Serve immediately with whole-grain bread, fruit, or beans. Top with optional sliced avocado and zucchini, if using.

Nutrition: Calories: 267 kcal; **Protein:** 23 g; **Carbohydrate:** 13 g; **Fat:** 17 g

Baked Eggs in Avocado

Preparation Time: 15 minutes
Cooking Time: 15 minutes
Servings: 2
Ingredients:
- 2 avocados
- Juice of 2 limes
- Black pepper, freshly ground
- 4 eggs
- 2 (8-inch) whole-wheat or corn tortillas, warmed
- **Optional for serving:** zucchini, halved, and cilantro, chopped

Directions:
1. Adjust the oven rack to the middle position and preheat the oven to 450°F. Scrape out the center of halved avocado using a spoon of about 1½ tbsp
2. Press lime juice over the avocados and season with black pepper to taste, and then place it on a baking sheet. Crack an egg into the avocado.
3. Bake within 10 to 15 minutes. Remove from oven and garnish with optional cilantro and zucchini and serve with warm tortillas.

Nutrition: Calories: 534 kcal; **Protein:** 18 g; **Carbohydrate:** 30 g; **Fat:** 29 g

Hearty Lentil Soup

Preparation Time: 15 minutes
Cooking Time: 30 minutes
Servings: 4

Ingredients:
- 1 tbsp olive oil
- 2 carrots, peeled and chopped
- 2 celery stalks, diced
- 1 tsp thyme, dried
- Black pepper, freshly ground
- 1 (28 oz.) can no-salt zucchini, diced and drained
- 1 cup dry lentils
- 5 cups water
- Salt

Directions:
1. Heat the oil in a large Dutch oven or pot over medium heat. Once the oil is simmering, add the carrot and celery. Cook, often stirring within 5 minutes.
2. Add the thyme and black pepper. Cook within 30 seconds. Pour in the drained diced zucchini and cook for a few more minutes, often stirring to enhance their flavor.
3. Put the lentils, water, plus a pinch of salt. Raise the heat then bring to a boil, then partially cover the pot and reduce heat to maintain a gentle simmer.
4. Cook within 30 minutes, or until lentils are tender but still hold their shape. Ladle into serving bowls and serve with a fresh green salad and whole-grain bread.

Nutrition: Calories: 168 kcal; **Protein:** 10 g; **Carbohydrate:** 35 g; **Fat:** 4 g

Loaded Baked Sweet Potatoes

Preparation Time: 15 minutes
Cooking Time: 20 minutes
Servings: 4
Ingredients:
- 4 sweet potatoes
- ½ cup non-fat or low-fat plain Greek yogurt
- Black pepper, freshly ground
- 1 tsp olive oil
- 1 red bell pepper, cored and diced
- 1 tsp cumin, ground
- 1 (15 oz.) can chickpeas, drained and rinsed

Directions:
1. Prick the potatoes using a fork and cook on your microwave's potato setting until potatoes are soft and cooked through, about 8 to 10 minutes for 4 potatoes. If you don't have a microwave, bake at 400°F for about 45 minutes.
2. Combine the yogurt and black pepper in a small bowl and mix well. Heat the oil in your

medium pot over medium heat. Add bell pepper, cumin, and additional black pepper to taste.
3. Add the chickpeas, stir to combine, and heat for about 5 minutes. Slice the potatoes lengthwise down the middle and top each half with a portion of the bean mixture followed by 1 to 2 tbsp of the yogurt. Serve immediately.

Nutrition: Calories: 264 kcal; **Protein:** 11 g; **Carbohydrate:** 51 g; **Fat:** 2 g

White Beans with Spinach and Pan-Roasted Zucchini

Preparation Time: 15 minutes
Cooking Time: 10 minutes
Servings: 2
Ingredients:
- 1 tbsp olive oil
- 4 small zucchini, halved lengthwise
- 10 oz. spinach, frozen, defrosted, and squeezed of excess water
- 2 tbsp water
- ¼ tsp black pepper, freshly ground
- 1 can white beans, drained

Directions:
1. Heat the oil in your large skillet over medium-high heat. Put the zucchini, cut-side down, and cook within 3 to 5 minutes; turn and cook within 1 minute more. Transfer to a plate.
2. Reduce heat to medium and add the spinach, water, and pepper to the skillet. Cook, tossing until the spinach is heated through, 2 to 3 minutes.
3. Return the zucchini to the skillet, put the white beans and toss until heated through 1 to 2 minutes.

Nutrition: Calories: 293 kcal; **Protein:** 15 g; **Carbohydrate:** 43 g; **Fat:** 9 g

Roasted Brussels Sprouts

Preparation Time: 5 minutes
Cooking Time: 20 minutes
Servings: 4
Ingredients:
- 1½ lb. Brussels sprouts, trimmed and halved
- 2 tbsp olive oil
- ¼ tsp salt
- ½ tsp black pepper, freshly ground

Directions:
1. Preheat the oven to 400°f. Combine the Brussels sprouts and olive oil in a large mixing bowl and toss until they are evenly coated.
2. Turn the Brussels sprouts out onto a large baking sheet and flip them over, so they are cut-side down with the flat part touching the baking sheet. Sprinkle with salt and pepper.
3. Bake within 20 to 30 minutes or until the Brussels sprouts are crisp and lightly charred on the outside and toasted on the bottom. The outer leaves will be extra dark, too. Serve immediately.

Nutrition: Calories: 134 kcal; **Protein:** 6 g; **Carbohydrate:** 15 g; **Fat:** 8 g

Stuffed Eggplant Shells

Preparation Time: 10 minutes
Cooking Time: 25 minutes
Servings: 2
Ingredients:
- 1 medium eggplant
- 1 cup water
- 1 tbsp olive oil
- 4 oz. white beans, cooked
- ½ cup green, red, or yellow bell peppers, chopped
- 1 cup zucchini, canned and unsalted
- ¼ cup celery, chopped
- 1 cup fresh mushrooms, sliced
- ¾ cup whole-wheat breadcrumbs
- Black pepper, freshly ground, to taste

Directions:
1. Prepare the oven to 350°F to preheat. Grease a baking dish with cooking spray and set it aside. Trim and cut the eggplant in half, lengthwise. Scoop out the pulp using a spoon and leave the shell about ¼ inch thick.
2. Place the shells in the baking dish with their cut side up. Add water to the bottom of the dish. Dice the eggplant pulp into cubes and set them aside. Add oil to an iron skillet and heat it over medium heat. Stir in peppers, chopped eggplant, zucchini, celery, and mushrooms.
3. Cook for 10 minutes on simmering heat, then stirs in beans, black pepper, and breadcrumbs. Divide this mixture into the eggplant shells. Cover the shells with a foil sheet and bake for 15 minutes. Serve warm.

Nutrition: Calories: 334 kcal; **Protein:** 2 g; **Carbohydrates:** 3 g; **Fat:** 1 g

Broccoli with Olive Oil

Preparation Time: 2 minutes
Cooking Time: 4 minutes
Servings: 4
Ingredients:
- 1 cup water
- 4 cups broccoli florets
- 1 tsp olive oil
- Salt
- Black pepper, freshly ground

Directions:
1. Put the broccoli in the boiling water in a small saucepan and cook for 2 to 3 minutes. The broccoli should retain its bright-green color. Drain the water from the broccoli.
2. Put the olive oil in a small sauté pan over medium-high heat. Sauté for 30 seconds. Put the broccoli, salt, plus pepper. Combine well and serve.

Nutrition: Calories: 38 kcal; **Protein:** 3 g; **Carbohydrate:** 5 g; **Fat:** 1 g

Grains, Beans, And Legumes

Bean and Spinach Casserole

Preparation Time: 20 minutes
Cooking Time: 30 minutes
Servings: 6
Ingredients:
- ½ cup whole-wheat bread crumbs
- 1 (15½ oz./ 439 g) can Great Northern beans
- 1 (15½ oz./ 439 g) can Navy beans
- 3 tbsp olive oil
- 2 carrots, chopped
- 1 celery stalk, chopped
- 1 cup baby spinach
- 3 zucchini, chopped
- 1 cup vegetable broth
- 1 tbsp parsley, chopped
- 1 tsp thyme, dried
- Sea salt and pepper to taste

Directions:
1. Preheat your oven to 380°F (193°C). Heat the oil in a skillet over medium heat.
2. Place in carrots, and celery. Sauté for 5 minutes.
3. Remove into a greased casserole.
4. Add in beans, spinach, zucchini, broth, parsley, thyme, salt, and pepper, and stir to combine.
5. Cover with foil then bake in the oven for 15 minutes. Take out the casserole from the oven, remove the foil, and spread the bread crumbs all over.
6. Bake for another 10 minutes until the top is crispy and golden. Serve warm.

Nutrition: Calories: 332 kcal; **Protein:** 16 g; **Carbohydrates:** 49 g; **Fat:** 8 g

Quinoa a la Puttanesca

Preparation Time: 20 minutes
Cooking Time: 15 minutes
Servings: 4
Ingredients:
- 1 cup brown quinoa
- 2 cups water

- Sea salt to taste
- 4 cups zucchini, diced
- 4 pitted green olives, sliced
- 4 Kalamata olives, sliced
- 1½ tbsp capers
- 1 tbsp olive oil
- 1 tbsp parsley, chopped
- ¼ cup basil, chopped

Directions:
1. Add quinoa, water, and salt to a medium pot and cook for 15 minutes. In a bowl, mix zucchini, green olives, olives, capers, olive oil, parsley, and basil.
2. Allow sitting for 5 minutes. Serve.

Nutrition: Calories: 231 kcal; **Protein:** 12 g; **Carbohydrates:** 35 g; **Fat:** 7 g

Hot Paprika Lentils

Preparation Time: 10 minutes
Cooking Time: 20 minutes
Servings: 6
Ingredients:
- 1 tbsp olive oil
- 1 tbsp hot paprika
- 2¼ cups lentils, drained
- ½ tsp thyme, dried
- Salt and black pepper, to taste

Directions:
1. Heat the oil in your pot over medium heat.
2. Sauté for 3 minutes. Add in paprika, salt, pepper, 5 cups water, lentils, and thyme.
3. Bring to a boil, lower the heat and simmer for 15 minutes, stirring often.

Nutrition: Calories: 111 kcal; **Protein:** 11 g; **Carbohydrates:** 9 g; **Fat:** 6 g

Herby Quinoa with Walnuts

Preparation Time: 20 minutes
Cooking Time: 10 to 15 minutes
Servings: 4
Ingredients:

- 2 zucchini, minced
- 1 cup quinoa
- 2 cups vegetable broth
- ¼ cup chives, chopped
- 2 tbsp parsley, chopped
- 2 tbsp basil, chopped
- 2 tbsp mint, chopped
- 1 tbsp olive oil
- 2 tbsp walnuts, minced

Directions:
1. In a pot, combine quinoa, vegetable broth.
2. Boil until the quinoa is tender and the liquid is absorbed, 10 to 15 minutes.
3. Stir in chives, parsley, basil, mint, zucchini, olive oil, zest, and walnuts. Warm for 5 minutes. Serve.

Nutrition: Calories: 308 kcal; **Protein:** 14 g; **Carbohydrates:** 31 g; **Fat:** 8 g

Tender Farro

Preparation Time: 8 minutes
Cooking Time: 40 minutes
Servings: 4
Ingredients:
- 1 cup farro
- 3 cups beef broth
- 1 tsp salt
- 1 tbsp almond butter
- 1 tbsp dried dill

Directions:
1. Place farro in the pan.
2. Add beef broth, dried dill, and salt.
3. Close the lid and place the mixture to boil.
4. Then boil it for 35 minutes over medium-low heat.
5. When the time is done, open the lid and add almond butter.
6. Mix up the cooked farro well.

Nutrition: Calories: 95 kcal; **Protein:** 6.4 g; **Carbohydrates:** 10.1 g; **Fat:** 3.3 g

Red Beans and Rice

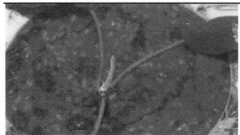

Preparation Time: 15 minutes
Cooking Time: 45 minutes
Servings: 2
Ingredients:

- ½ cup dry brown rice
- 1 cup water, plus ¼ cup
- 1 can red beans, drained
- 1 tbsp cumin, ground
- Juice of 1 lime
- 4 handfuls fresh spinach
- **Optional toppings:** avocado, zucchini, chopped; Greek yogurt

Directions:
1. Mix rice plus water in a pot and bring to a boil. Cover then place heat to a low simmer. Cook within 30 to 40 minutes or according to package directions.
2. Meanwhile, add the beans, ¼ cup of water, cumin, and lime juice to a medium skillet. Simmer within 5 to 7 minutes.
3. Once the liquid is mostly gone, remove from the heat and add the spinach. Cover and let spinach wilt slightly, 2 to 3 minutes. Mix in with the beans. Serve beans with rice. Add toppings, if using.

Nutrition: Calories: 232 kcal; **Protein:** 13 g; **Carbohydrate:** 41 g; **Fat:** 2 g

Chicken Green Beans Soup

Preparation Time: 5 minutes
Cooking Time: 25 minutes
Servings: 4
Ingredients:
- 1 lb. chicken breasts, boneless, skinless, cubed
- 1 ½ cups celery, chopped
- 1 tbsp olive oil
- 1 cup carrots, chopped
- 1 cup green beans, chopped
- 3 tbsp flour
- 1 tsp oregano, dried
- 2 tsp basil, dried
- ¼ tsp nutmeg
- 1 tsp thyme
- 32 oz. chicken broth
- ½ cup almond milk
- 2 cups green peas, frozen
- ¼ tsp black pepper

Directions:
1. Add the chicken to a skillet and sauté for 6 minutes, then remove it from the heat.
2. Warm up the olive oil in a pan and stir in the carrots, flour, green beans, basil, sautéed chicken, thyme, oregano, and nutmeg.
3. Sauté for approximately 3 minutes, then transfer the ingredients to a large pan.

4. Add the milk and broth and cook until it boils.
5. Stir in the green peas and cook for 5 minutes.
6. Adjust seasoning with pepper and serve warm.

Nutrition: Calories: 277 kcal; **Protein:** 25.5 g; **Carbohydrates:** 17.3 g; **Fat:** 7.6 g

Brown Rice Pilaf

Preparation Time: 5 minutes
Cooking Time: 10 minutes
Servings: 4
Ingredients:
- 1 cup low-sodium vegetable broth
- ½ tbsp olive oil
- 1 scallion, thinly sliced
- 1 cup instant brown rice
- ⅛ tsp black pepper, freshly ground

Directions:
1. Mix the vegetable broth, olive oil, and scallion in a saucepan and boil. Put rice, then boil it again, adjust the heat and simmer within 10 minutes.
2. Remove and let stand within 5 minutes. Fluff with a fork then season with black pepper.

Nutrition: Calories: 100 kcal; **Protein:** 2 g; **Carbohydrate:** 19 g; **Fat:** 2 g

Southern Bean Bowl

Preparation Time: 15 minutes
Cooking Time: 0 minutes
Servings: 4
Ingredients:
- 1 zucchini, chopped
- 1 red bell pepper, chopped
- 1green bell pepper, chopped
- 1 (14½ oz./411 g) can black-eyed peas
- 1 (14½ oz./411 g) can black beans
- ¼ cup capers
- 2 avocados, pitted
- ¼ cup sake
- 1 tsp oregano, dried
- Sea salt, to taste
- 2 tbsp olive oil
- 1 cup leafy greens, chopped

Directions:
1. In a bowl, mix the zucchini, peppers, black-eyed peas, beans, and capers.
2. Put the avocados, sake, olive oil, oregano, and salt in a food processor and blitz until

smooth. Add the dressing to the bean bowl and toss to combine.
3. Top with leafy greens to serve.

Nutrition: Calories: 412 kcal; **Protein:** 7 g; **Carbohydrates:** 48 g; **Fat:** 16 g

Hot Coconut Beans with Vegetables

Preparation Time: 15 minutes
Cooking Time: 10 minutes
Servings: 4
Ingredients:
- 2 tbsp olive oil
- 1 red bell pepper, chopped
- 1 tbsp hot powder
- 1 (13½ oz./383 g) can coconut milk
- 2 (15½ oz./439 g) cans white beans
- 1 (14½ oz./411 g) can zucchini, diced
- 3 cups fresh baby spinach
- Sea salt and pepper, to taste
- Walnuts, chopped and toasted

Directions:
1. Heat the oil in your pot over medium heat. Place in hot powder, and bell pepper and sauté for 5 minutes, stirring occasionally.
2. Put in the coconut milk and whisk until well mixed.
3. Add in white beans, zucchini, spinach, salt, and pepper, and cook for 5 minutes until the spinach wilts.
4. Garnish with walnuts and serve.

Nutrition: Calories: 578 kcal; **Protein:** 11 g; **Carbohydrates:** 48 g; **Fat:** 38 g

Quinoa Salmon Bowl

Preparation Time: 15 minutes
Cooking Time: 0 minutes
Servings: 4
Ingredients:
- 4 cups cooked quinoa
- 1 lb. (45g;) salmon, cooked and flaked

- 3 cups arugula
- 6 radishes, thinly sliced
- 1 zucchini, sliced into half moons
- 3 scallions, minced
- 2 tbsp almond oil
- 1 tbsp apple cider vinegar
- 1 tsp Sriracha or other hot sauce (or more if you like it spicy)
- 1 tsp salt
- ½ cup almonds, toasted and slivered (optional)

Directions:
1. Combine the quinoa, salmon, arugula, radishes, zucchini, and scallions in a large bowl.
2. Add the almond oil, vinegar, Sriracha, and salt and mix well.
3. Divide the mixture among four serving bowls, garnish with the toasted almonds (if using), and serve.

Nutrition: Calories: 790 kcal; **Protein:** 37 g; **Carbohydrates:** 45 g; **Fat:** 22 g

Fiery Quinoa

Preparation Time: 10 minutes
Cooking Time: 20 minutes
Servings: 4
Ingredients:
- 1 cup quinoa, rinsed
- 2 cups water
- ½ cup coconut, shredded
- ¼ cup hemp seeds
- 2 tbsp flaxseed
- 1 tsp cinnamon, ground
- 1 tsp vanilla extract
- Pinch sea salt
- 1 cup fresh berries of your choice, divided
- ¼ cup hazelnuts, chopped

Directions:
1. Combine the quinoa and water in a medium saucepan over high heat.
2. Bring to a boil, then place the heat to a simmer, and cook for 15 to 20 minutes, or until the quinoa is cooked through. It should double or triple in bulk to couscous, and be slightly translucent.
3. Stir in the coconut, hemp seeds, flaxseed, cinnamon, vanilla, and salt.
4. Divide the quinoa among four bowls and top each serving with ¼ cup of berries and 1 tbsp of hazelnuts.

Nutrition: Calories: 286 kcal; **Protein:** 10 g; **Carbohydrates:** 32 g; **Fat:** 13 g

Chunky Black-Bean Dip

Preparation Time: 5 minutes
Cooking Time: 1 minute
Servings: 2
Ingredients:
- 1 (15 oz.) can black beans, drained, with liquid reserved
- ½-can chipotle peppers in adobo sauce
- ¼ cup plain Greek yogurt
- Black pepper, freshly ground

Directions:
1. Combine beans, peppers, and yogurt in a food processor or blender and process until smooth.
2. Add some of the bean liquid, 1 tbsp at a time, for a thinner consistency.
3. Season to taste with black pepper.
4. Serve.

Nutrition: Calories: 70 kcal; **Protein:** 8 g; **Carbohydrate:** 11 g; **Fat:** 3 g

Black-Bean Soup

Preparation Time: 15 minutes
Cooking Time: 20 minutes
Servings: 4
Ingredients:
- 1 tbsp olive oil
- 2 cans black beans, drained
- 1 cup fresh zucchini, diced
- 5 cups low-sodium vegetable broth
- ¼ tsp black pepper, freshly ground
- ¼ cup fresh cilantro, chopped

Directions:
1. Put the olive oil in a large saucepan over medium heat for 4 minutes
2. Put the black beans, zucchini, vegetable broth, and black pepper. Boil, then adjust heat to simmer within 15 minutes.
3. Remove, then work in batches, ladle the soup into a blender, and process until somewhat smooth. Put it back into the pot, add the cilantro, and heat until warmed through. Serve immediately.

Nutrition: Calories: 234 kcal; **Protein:** 11 g; **Carbohydrate:** 37 g; **Fat:** 5 g

Asparagus Rice

Preparation Time: 20 minutes
Cooking Time: 10 minutes
Servings: 4
Ingredients:

- 3 large eggs, beaten
- ½ tsp ginger, ground
- 2 tsp low-sodium soy sauce
- 2 tbsp olive oil
- 1 cup cremini mushrooms, sliced
- 1 (10 oz.) package brown rice, frozen and thawed
- 8 oz. fresh asparagus, about 15 spears, cut into 1-inch pieces
- 1 tsp sesame oil

Directions:

1. Whisk the eggs, ginger, and soy sauce in a small bowl and set aside.
2. Heat the olive oil in a medium skillet or wok over medium heat.
3. Sauté for 2 minutes until tender-crisp.
4. Add the mushrooms and rice; stir-fry for 3 minutes longer.
5. Add the asparagus and fry for 2 minutes.
6. Move the rice mixture to one side of the skillet and pour in the egg mixture. Stir the eggs until cooked through, 2 to 3 minutes, and stir into the rice mixture.
7. Sprinkle the fried rice with the sesame oil and serve.

Nutrition: Calories: 247 kcal; **Protein:** 9 g; **Carbohydrates:** 25 g; **Fat:** 13 g

Jalapeno Black-Eyed Peas Mix

Preparation Time: 10 minutes
Cooking Time: 5 hours
Servings: 12
Ingredients:

- 17 oz. black-eyed peas
- 1 sweet red pepper, chopped
- 1 jalapeno, chopped
- 6 cups water
- ½ tsp cumin, ground
- A pinch black pepper
- 2 tbsp cilantro, chopped

Directions:

1. In a slow cooker, mix the peas with the red pepper, jalapeno, black pepper, cumin, water, and cilantro, cover, and cook low for 5 hours.
2. Serve.

Nutrition: Calories: 75 kcal; **Protein:** 4.3 g; **Carbohydrates:** 7.2 g; **Fat:** 3.5 g

Healthy Vegetable Fried Rice

Preparation Time: 15 minutes
Cooking Time: 10 minutes
Servings: 4
Ingredients:
For the sauce:

- 1 tbsp dark molasses

For the fried rice:

- 1 tsp olive oil
- 2 whole eggs, lightly beaten + 4 egg whites
- 1 cup mixed vegetables, frozen
- 1 cup edamame, frozen
- 2 cups brown rice, cooked

Directions:

1. Prepare the sauce by combining the molasses in a glass jar. Shake well.
2. Heat-up oil in a large wok or skillet over medium-high heat. Add eggs and egg whites, and let cook until the eggs set, for about 1 minute.
3. Break up eggs with a spatula or spoon into small pieces. Add frozen mixed vegetables and frozen edamame. Cook for 4 minutes, stirring frequently.
4. Add the brown rice and sauce to the vegetable-and-egg mixture. Cook for 5 minutes or until heated through. Serve immediately.

Nutrition: Calories: 210 kcal; **Protein:** 13 g; **Carbohydrate:** 28 g; **Fat:** 6 g

Vegan Bean Mix

Preparation Time: 10 minutes
Cooking Time: 0 minutes
Servings:
INGREDIENTS:

- 1 cup lettuce, chopped
- 1 cucumber, chopped

- ½ cup corn kernels, cooked
- ½ cup fresh parsley, chopped
- 1 cup black beans, cooked

DIRECTION:
1. Put all ingredients in the mixing bowl and carefully mix.
2. Then transfer the mix in the serving bowls.
3. Add olive oil, if desired.

NUTRITION: Calories: 227; Protein: 9.3g; Fat: 19.3g

Stir-Fried Green Beans

Preparation Time: 10 minutes
Cooking Time: 20 minutes
Servings: 3
INGREDIENTS:
- 1-pound green beans
- 1 tablespoon olive oil
- 1 teaspoon allspices
- ¼ cup of water
- 1 teaspoon apple cider vinegar

DIRECTION:
1. Chop the green beans roughly and put them in the hot saucepan.
2. Add water and cook the vegetables for 10 minutes on low heat.
3. Add olive oil, allspices, and stir well.
4. Cook the green beans for 10 minutes more.
5. When the vegetables are soft, they are cooked.
6. Sprinkle the beans with apple cider vinegar and transfer in the plates.

NUTRITION: Calories: 366; Protein: 12.3g; Carbs: 33.4g; Fat: 19.3g

Poultry

Roasted chicken

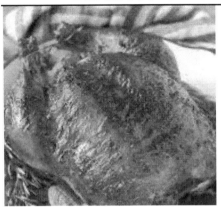

Preparation time: 65 minutes
Cooking time: 70 minutes
Serving: 6
INGREDIENTS:
1. 1 whole roasted chicken, about 6–7 pounds
2. 1–1 1/2 tsp. Kosher salt
3. 1/4 tsp. Black pepper

DIRECTIONS:
2. Preheat oven to 450 degrees f. Remove and discard giblets and neck from chicken cavity. Rinse chicken in several changes of cold water and pat dry.
3. Rub skin and flesh with kosher salt and black pepper. Place on roasting rack in pan. Transfer to oven and roast the juices run clear from the breast and the leg moves easily and the internal temperature are about 160 degrees, about 70 minutes (10 minutes per pound).

NUTRITION (PER SERVING): Calories: 235 Total fat: 6 g   Protein: 42 g.

Healthy Chicken Orzo

Preparation Time: 15 minutes
Cooking Time: 15 minutes
Servings: 4
Ingredients:
- 1 cup whole wheat orzo
- 1 lb. chicken breasts, sliced
- ½ tsp red pepper flakes
- ½ cup feta cheese, crumbled
- ½ tsp oregano
- 1 tbsp fresh parsley, chopped
- 1 tbsp fresh basil, chopped
- ¼ cup pine nuts

- 1 cup spinach, chopped
- ¼ cup white wine
- ½ cup olives, sliced
- 1 cup zucchini, cut in half
- 2 tbsp olive oil
- ½ tsp pepper
- ½ tsp salt

Directions:
1. Add water to a small saucepan and bring to boil. Heat 1 tbsp of olive oil in a pan over medium heat. Season chicken with pepper and salt and cook in the pan for 5–7 minutes on each side. Remove from pan and set aside.
2. Add orzo to boiling water and cook according to the packet directions. Heat remaining olive oil in a pan on medium heat, then sauté for a minute. Stir in white wine and zucchini and cook on high for 3 minutes.
3. Add cooked orzo, spices, spinach, pine nuts, and olives and stir until well combined. Add chicken on top of orzo and sprinkle with feta cheese. Serve and enjoy.

Nutrition: Calories: 518 kcal; **Fat:** 12.7 g; **Protein:** 20.6 g; **Carbs:** 26.2 g

Turkey meatloaf

Preparation time: 35 minutes
Cooking time: 1 hour 25 minutes
Serving: 10
INGREDIENTS:
7. 1 tsp. Olive oil
8. 1 tsp. Dried Greek oregano
9. 2–3 tbsp. Dijon mustard

49

10. 1/2 tsp. Black pepper
11. 1/2 tsp. Salt
12. ½ c. Chopped fresh italian flat leaf parsley leaves
13. 2 slices good quality white bread
14. ½ c. Beef or chicken stock none fat
15. 1 large egg, lightly beaten
16. 2 pounds lean ground chicken or turkey

DIRECTIONS:

7. Preheat the oven to 350°f. Lightly grease an 8 x 4-inch loaf pan.
8. Place a medium size skillet over low heat and when it is hot, add the oil. Add the oregano and cook for about 10 minutes. Transfer to a large mixing bowl and set aside to cool. In the meantime, soak the bread in the stock until it is moist, about 2 minutes. Drain off as much liquid as possible. Add the bread to the cooled mixture.
9. Add the eggs and ground meat and mix, by hand, until everything is thoroughly incorporated. Place the mixture in the prepared loaf pan, transfer to the oven and cook for about 1 hour and 15 minutes.

NUTRITION (PER SERVING): Calories: 162 Total fat: 16 g Protein: 14 g.

Mediterranean Turkey Breast

Preparation Time: 15 minutes
Cooking Time: 4 minutes and 30 minutes
Servings: 6
Ingredients:

- 4 lb. turkey breast
- 3 tbsp flour
- ¾ cup chicken stock
- 1 tsp oregano, dried
- ½ cup zucchini, chopped
- ½ cup olives, chopped
- ¼ tsp pepper
- ½ tsp salt

Directions:

1. Add turkey breast, oregano, zucchini, olives, pepper, and salt to the slow cooker. Add half stock. Cook on high within 4 hours.
2. Whisk remaining stock and flour in a small bowl and add to slow cooker. Cover and cook for 30 minutes more. Serve and enjoy.

Nutrition: Calories: 537 kcal; **Fat:** 9.7 g; **Protein:** 59.1 g; **Carbs:** 29.6 g

Vietnamese style chicken

Preparation time: 30 minutes
Cooking time: 20 minutes
Serving: 4
INGREDIENTS:

1. 2 tbsp. Plus 1/3 cup water
2. ¼ c. Asian fish sauce
3. 1 ½ pounds boneless skinless chicken breasts (2 large), each breast half cut in half
4. A of Pinch black pepper
5. ¼ c. Chopped fresh basil or cilantro leaves

DIRECTIONS:

1. Set aside the 2 tablespoons water and the Asian fish sauce in a small bowl. Set aside the shallots, and black pepper in a separate small bowl.
2. In a big skillet, combine the remaining 1/3 cup water and cook with a medium heat for 6 minutes, or until the sugar has caramelized into a deep brown color.
3. Remove the pan from the heat and carefully pour in the fish sauce mixture (to minimize splattering). Return to the fire and continue to simmer until the mixture reaches a boil. Time: 1–2 minutes Add the shallot mixture and simmer for 3 minutes, or until the shallots have softened.
4. Cook and tossing occasionally, until the chicken is cooked through, about 4 minutes per side, in a single layer. Serve immediately with a basil garnish.

NUTRITION (PER SERVING): Calories: 374 Total fat: 8 Protein 58 g.

Pan grilled chicken with basil

Preparation time: 2 hours
Cooking time: 10 minutes
Serving: 4
INGREDIENTS:

1. 1 ½ pounds boneless, skinless chicken breasts, pounded thin and sliced lengthwise to get 4 cutlets
2. ¼ c. Chopped fresh basil leaves
3. 1 tsp. Dried oregano
4. ½ tsp. Black pepper
5. ½ tsp. Kosher salt

DIRECTIONS:

6. Place the chicken, basil and oregano in a non-reactive glass or ceramic bowl and mix to combine. Cover and refrigerate at least 2 but no more than 4 hours.
7. Drain the chicken and discard the marinade. Sprinkle with the salt and pepper. Place a large cast iron skillet over medium high heat and when it is almost smoking hot, add the chicken, waiting for the pan to reheat between additions. Cook until golden brown, just firm to the touch and cooked throughout, about 4 minutes per side, depending on the thickness of the chicken.

NUTRITION (PER SERVING): Calories: 324
Total fat: 8 g Protein: 37 g.

Chicken

Preparation Time: 15 minutes
Cooking Time: 12 minutes
Servings: 3
Ingredients:

- 3 chicken breasts, cut into thin slices
- 2 tbsp olive oil
- Pepper
- Salt

Directions:

1. Warm-up olive oil in a pan over medium heat. Sauté for 30 seconds. Put the chicken in the pan and sauté within 10 minutes. Bring to boil. Remove from heat and season with pepper and salt. Serve and enjoy.

Nutrition: Calories: 439 kcal; **Fat:** 17.8 g; **Protein:** 42.9 g; **Carbs:** 4.9 g

Tuscan chicken

Preparation time: 5 minutes
Cooking time: 20 minutes
Serving: 4

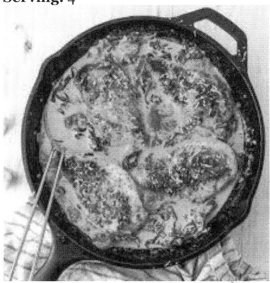

INGREDIENTS:

- 4 boneless, skinless chicken breast halves, pounded to ½–to ¾-inch thickness
- ½ tsp. Sea salt
- 1/8 tsp. Freshly ground black pepper
- 2 tbsp. Extra-virgin olive oil
- 3 zucchini, chopped
- ½ c. Sliced green olives
- ¼ c. Dry white wine

DIRECTIONS:

- Season the chicken breasts with the salt, and pepper.
- In a large nonstick skillet over medium-high heat, heat the olive oil until it shimmers. Add the chicken and cook 7 to 10 minutes per side, until it reaches an internal temperature of 165°f. Remove the chicken and set aside on a platter, tented with foil.
- In the same skillet, add the zucchini, and olives. Cook for about 4 minutes, stirring occasionally, until the zucchini is tender.

- Add the white wine and use a wooden spoon to scrape any browned bits from the bottom of the pan. Simmer for 1 minute. Return the chicken and any juices that have collected on the platter to the pan and stir to coat with the sauce and vegetables.

NUTRITION (PER SERVING): Calories: 171 Total fat: 11 g Protein: 28

Chicken cacciatore

Preparation time: 10 minutes
Cooking time: 20 minutes
Serving: 4
INGREDIENTS:

1. 2 tbsp. Extra-virgin olive oil
2. 1½ pounds boneless skinless chicken breasts, cut into bite-size pieces
3. 2 (28-ounce) cans crushed zucchini, drained
4. ½ c. Black olives, chopped
5. 1/2 tsp. Sea salt
6. 1/8 tsp. Freshly ground black pepper

DIRECTIONS:

7. In a large nonstick skillet over medium to high heat, heat the olive oil until it shimmers.
8. Add the chicken and cook for 7 to 10 minutes, stirring occasionally, until it is browned.
9. Stir in the zucchini, olives, salt, and pepper. Simmer for 10 minutes, stirring occasionally.

Variation tip: chop ¼ cup fresh basil leaves and stir them in just before serving for a fresh, herbal flavor.

NUTRITION (PER SERVING): Calories: 305 Total fat: 11 g Total carbs: 34 g Fiber: 13 g Protein: 19 g

Chicken adobo

Preparation time: 10 minutes
Cooking time: 15 minutes
Serving: 4
INGREDIENTS:

- 3 tbsp. Extra-virgin olive oil
- 1½ pounds boneless skinless chicken breasts, cut into bite-size pieces
- 2 tsp. Ground turmeric
- ¼ c. Low-sodium soy sauce
- ½ tsp. Sea salt
- ¼ tsp. Freshly ground black pepper

DIRECTIONS:

4. In a large nonstick skillet over medium to high heat, heat the olive oil until it shimmers.
5. Add the chicken and turmeric. Cook for like 7 to 10 minutes, stirring occasionally, until the chicken is cooked through.
6. Stir in the soy sauce, salt, and pepper. Cook for 3 minutes, stirring.

Ingredient tip: let's talk about freshly ground black pepper. While it's not a requirement in these recipes, grinding black peppercorns fresh produces a lot more flavor. Plus, grinding pepper makes your cooking feel more immediate, like you're a celebrity chef prepping food on tv. You can even find peppercorns in a disposable grinder in the spice aisle of your local grocery store.

NUTRITION (PER SERVING): Calories: 498 Total fat: 22 g Total carbs: 11 Protein: 46 g.

Chicken and bell pepper sauté

Preparation time: 15 minutes
Cooking time: 15 minutes
Serving: 4

INGREDIENTS:
1. 3 tbsp. Extra-virgin olive oil
2. 1 red bell pepper, chopped
3. 1½ pounds boneless, skinless chicken breasts, cut into bite-size pieces
4. ½ tsp. Sea salt
5. ¼ tsp. Freshly ground black pepper

DIRECTIONS:
7. In a large nonstick skillet over medium-high heat, heat the olive oil until it shimmers.
8. Add the red bell pepper and chicken. Cook for 10 minutes, stirring it occasionally.
9. Add salt and pepper. Cook for 30 seconds, stirring constantly.

Ingredient tip: remember, smaller pieces cook faster. Cut the chicken and veggies into same-size pieces (½ to 1 inch) so they cook evenly.

NUTRITION (PER SERVING): Calories: 279 Total fat: 13 g Protein: 23

Baked Chicken

Preparation Time: 15 minutes
Cooking Time: 35 minutes
Servings: 4
Ingredients:
- 2 lb. chicken tenders
- 2 large zucchini
- 2 tbsp olive oil
- 3 dill sprigs

For topping:
- 2 tbsp low-fat feta cheese, crumbled
- 1 tbsp olive oil
- 1 tbsp fresh dill, chopped

Directions:
1. Warm oven to 200°C/400°F. Drizzle the olive oil on a baking tray, then place chicken, zucchini, and dill, on the tray. Season with salt. Bake chicken within 30 minutes.

2. Meanwhile, in a small bowl, stir all topping ingredients. Place chicken on the serving tray, then top with veggies and discard dill sprigs. Sprinkle topping mixture on top of chicken and vegetables. Serve and enjoy.

Nutrition: Calories: 557 kcal; **Fat:** 23.6 g; **Protein:** 47.9 g; **Carbs:** 5.2 g

Teriyaki chicken under pressure

Preparation time: 25 minutes
Cooking time: 20 minutes
Servings: 8
INGREDIENTS:
- 1 c. chicken broth
- 1tbsp brown sugar
- 2 tbsp. ground ginger
- 1 tsp. pepper
- 3 pounds boneless and skinless chicken thighs
- ¼ c. apple cider vinegar
- ¾ c. low-sodium soy sauce
- 20 ounces canned pineapple, crushed

DIRECTIONS:
7. Place the chicken in your Instant Pot.
8. Combine all of the remaining ingredients in a bowl.
9. Pour the sauce over the meat.
10. Seal the lid, select MANUAL, and cook for 20 minutes on high pressure.
11. Once cooking is complete, select Cancel and perform a quick release.
12. Serve and enjoy.

NUTRITION (PER SERVING): Calories: 352 Carbs: 31 g Fiber: 1.2 g Fat: 11.4 g Protein: 30.7 g.

Chicken-Apple Sausage

Preparation Time: 15 minutes or fewer
Cooking Time: 6 to 8 hours on low
Portions: 4–6
INGREDIENTS:
1. 1-pound ground chicken
2. ½ medium apple, peeled and minced
3. 1 tsp. sea salt
4. ½ tsp. dried parsley flakes
5. ½ tsp. dried basil leaves
6. ¼ tsp. ground cinnamon

DIRECTION:
- In a large bowl, combine the chicken, apple, salt, pepper, parsley flakes, basil, and cinnamon. Mix well. Press the chicken mixture into the bottom of your slow cooker, ensuring it's a thin layer throughout.
- Cover the cooker and set to low. Cook for 6 to 8 hours, or until the meat is completely cooked through.
- Using a silicone spatula, loosen the chicken from around the edges and transfer to a cutting board. Cut into desired shapes (sticks or circles are common) and serve.

Make-ahead tip: Make a full batch of these to freeze for later. Keep in an airtight container and, when you're ready to eat, heat the sausage (no need to thaw) in a skillet over medium-low heat for 8 to 10 minutes, turning often.
NUTRITION: Calories: 210 Total Fat: 12 g Total Carbohydrates: 4 g Sugar: 2 g Fiber: 1 g Protein: 21 g Sodium: 0.672 g.

Simple Mediterranean Chicken

Preparation Time: 15 minutes
Cooking Time: 15 minutes
Servings: 3
Ingredients:
- 2 chicken breasts, skinless and boneless
- 1 ½ cup zucchini, cut in half

- ½ cup olives
- 2 tbsp olive oil
- 1 tsp Italian seasoning
- ¼ tsp pepper
- ¼ tsp salt

Directions:
1. Season chicken with Italian seasoning, pepper, and salt. Warm-up olive oil in a pan over medium heat. Add season chicken to the pan and cook for 4–6 minutes on each side. Transfer chicken to a plate.
2. Put zucchini plus olives in the pan and cook for 2–4 minutes. Pour olive and zucchini mixture on top of the chicken and serve.

Nutrition: Calories: 468 kcal; **Fat:** 19.4 g; **Protein:** 33.8 g; **Carbs:** 7.8 g

Roasted Chicken Thighs

Preparation Time: 15 minutes
Cooking Time: 55 minutes
Servings: 4
Ingredients:
- 8 chicken thighs
- 3 tbsp fresh parsley, chopped
- 1 tsp oregano, dried
- ¼ cup capers, drained
- 10 oz. red peppers, roasted and sliced
- 2 cups zucchini
- 1 ½ lb. potatoes, cut into small chunks
- 3 tbsp olive oil
- Pepper
- Salt

Directions:
1. Warm oven to 200–400°F. Season chicken with pepper and salt. Heat 2 tbsp of olive oil in a pan over medium heat. Add chicken to the pan and sear until lightly golden brown from all sides.
2. Transfer chicken onto a baking tray. Add zucchini, potatoes, capers, oregano and red peppers around the chicken. Season with pepper and salt and drizzle with remaining

olive oil. Bake in preheated oven for 45–55 minutes. Garnish with parsley and serve.

Nutrition: Calories: 548 kcal; **Fat:** 19.1 g; **Protein:** 31.3 g; **Carbs:** 45.2 g

Pepper Chicken

Preparation Time: 15 minutes
Cooking Time: 21 minutes
Servings: 2
Ingredients:

- 2 chicken breasts, cut into strips
- 2 bell peppers, cut into strips
- 3 tbsp water
- 2 tbsp olive oil
- 1 tbsp paprika
- 1 tsp black pepper
- ½ tsp salt

Directions:

1. Warm-up olive oil in a large saucepan over medium heat. Sauté for 2–3 minutes. Add peppers and cook for 3 minutes. Add chicken and spices and stir to coat. Add water and stir well. Bring to boil. Cover and simmer for 10–15 minutes. Serve and enjoy.

Nutrition: Calories: 462 kcal; **Fat:** 20.7 g; **Protein:** 44.7 g; **Carbs:** 14.8 g

Mustard Chicken Tenders

Preparation Time: 15 minutes
Cooking Time: 20 minutes
Servings: 4
Ingredients:

- 1 lb. chicken tenders
- 2 tbsp fresh tarragon, chopped
- ¼ cup whole grain mustard
- ½ tsp paprika
- ½ tsp pepper
- ¼ tsp kosher salt

Directions:

1. Warm oven to 425°F. Add all ingredients except chicken to the large bowl and mix well. Put the chicken in the bowl, then stir until well coated. Place chicken on a baking dish and cover. Bake within 15–20 minutes. Serve and enjoy.

Nutrition: Calories: 242 kcal; **Fat:** 9.5 g; **Protein:** 33.2 g; **Carbs:** 3.1 g

Chicken with Mushrooms

Preparation Time: 15 minutes
Cooking Time: 6 hours and 10 minutes
Servings: 2
Ingredients:

- 2 chicken breasts, skinless and boneless
- 1 cup mushrooms, sliced
- 1 cup chicken stock
- ½ tsp thyme, dried
- Pepper
- Salt

Directions:

1. Add all ingredients to the slow cooker. Cook on low within 6 hours. Serve and enjoy.

Nutrition: Calories: 313 kcal; **Fat:** 11.3 g; **Protein:** 44.3 g; **Carbs:** 6.9 g

Honey Crusted Chicken

Preparation Time: 10 minutes
Cooking Time: 25 minutes
Servings: 2
Ingredients:

- 1 tsp paprika
- 8 saltine crackers, 2 inches square
- 2 chicken breasts, each 4 oz.
- 4 tsp honey

Directions:

1. Set the oven to heat at 375°F. Grease a baking dish with cooking oil. Smash the crackers in a Ziplock bag and toss them with paprika in a bowl. Brush chicken with honey and add it to the crackers.
2. Mix well and transfer the chicken to the baking dish. Bake the chicken for 25 minutes until golden brown. Serve.

Nutrition: Calories: 219 kcal; **Fat:** 17 g; **Carbs:** 12.1 g; **Protein:** 31 g

Chicken Sliders

Preparation Time: 10 minutes
Cooking Time: 10 minutes
Servings: 4

Ingredients:

- 10 oz. chicken breast, ground
- 1 tbsp black pepper
- 1 tbsp balsamic vinegar
- 1 tbsp fennel seed, crushed
- 4 whole-wheat mini buns
- 4 lettuce leaves
- 4 zucchini slices

Directions:

1. Combine all the ingredients except the wheat buns, zucchini, and lettuce. Mix well and refrigerate the mixture for 1 hour. Divide the mixture into 4 patties.
2. Broil these patties in a greased baking tray until golden brown. Place the chicken patties in the wheat buns along with lettuce and zucchini. Serve.

Nutrition: Calories: 224 kcal; **Fat:** 4.5 g; **Carbs:** 10.2 g; **Protein:** 67.4 g

Paella with Chicken, Leeks, and Tarragon

Preparation Time: 10 minutes
Cooking Time: 20 minutes
Servings: 2
Ingredients:

- 1 tsp extra-virgin olive oil
- 2 leeks (whites only), thinly sliced
- 1 lb. chicken breast, boneless, skinless, cut into strips ½-inch-wide and 2 inches long
- 2 large zucchini, chopped
- 1 red pepper, sliced
- ⅔ cup long-grain brown rice
- 1 tsp tarragon, or to taste
- 2 cups fat-free, unsalted chicken broth
- 1 cup peas, frozen
- ¼ cup fresh parsley, chopped

Directions:

1. Preheat a nonstick pan with olive oil over medium heat. Toss in leeks, chicken strips. Sauté for 5 minutes. Stir in red pepper slices and zucchini. Stir and cook for 5 minutes.
2. Add tarragon, broth, and rice. Let it boil, then reduce the heat to a simmer. Continue

cooking for 10 minutes, then add peas and continue cooking until the liquid is thoroughly cooked. Garnish with parsley and serve.

Nutrition: Calories: 388 kcal; **Fat:** 15.2 g; **Carbs:** 5.4 g; **Protein:** 27 g

Stuffed Chicken Breasts

Preparation Time: 15 minutes
Cooking Time: 30 minutes
Servings: 4
Ingredients:

- 3 tbsp raisins, seedless
- ½ cup celery, chopped
- 1 bay leaf
- 1 cup apple with peel, chopped
- 2 tbsp water chestnuts, chopped
- 4 large chicken breast halves, 5 oz. each
- 1 tbsp olive oil
- 1 cup fat-free milk
- 1 tbsp all-purpose organic whole wheat flour

Directions:

1. Set the oven to heat at 425°F. Grease a baking dish with cooking oil. Soak raisins in warm water until they swell. Grease a heated skillet with cooking spray.
2. Add celery, and bay leaf. Sauté for 5 minutes. Discard the bay leaf, then toss in apples. Stir and cook for 2 minutes. Drain the soaked raisin and pat them dry to remove excess water.
3. Add raisins and water chestnuts to the apple mixture. Pull apart the chicken's skin and stuff the apple raisin mixture between the skin and the chicken. Preheat olive oil in another skillet and sear the breasts for 5 minutes per side.
4. Place the chicken breasts in the baking dish and cover the dish. Bake for 15 minutes until the temperature reaches 165°F. Prepare sauce by mixing milk, flour, in a saucepan.
5. Stir and cook until the mixture thickens, about 5 minutes. Pour this sauce over the

baked chicken. Bake again in the covered dish for 10 minutes. Serve.

Nutrition: Calories: 357 kcal; **Fat:** 32.7 g; **Carbs:** 17.7 g; **Protein:** 31.2 g

Apricot Chicken

Preparation Time: 15 minutes
Cooking Time: 6 minutes
Servings: 4
Ingredients:
- 1 bottle creamy French dressing
- ¼ cup flavorless oil
- White rice, cooked
- 1 large jar Apricot preserve
- 4 lb. chicken, boneless and skinless

Directions:
1. Rinse and pat dry the chicken. Dice into bite-size pieces. In a large bowl, mix the apricot preserve and creamy dressing. Stir until thoroughly combined. Place the chicken in the bowl. Mix until coated.
2. In a large skillet, heat the oil. Place the chicken in the oil gently. Cook 4–6 minutes on each side, until golden brown. Serve over rice.

Nutrition: Calories: 202 kcal; **Fat:** 12 g; **Carbs:** 75 g; **Protein:** 20 g

Buffalo Chicken Salad Wrap

Preparation Time: 10 minutes
Cooking Time: 10 minutes
Servings: 4
Ingredients:
- 3–4 oz. chicken breasts
- 2 whole chipotle peppers
- ¼ cup white wine vinegar
- ¼ cup low-calorie mayonnaise
- 2 stalks celery, diced
- 2 carrots, cut into matchsticks
- ½ cup rutabaga or another root vegetable, thinly sliced
- 4 oz. spinach, cut into strips
- 2 whole-grain tortillas (12-inch diameter)

Directions:
1. Set the oven or a grill to heat at 375°F. Bake the chicken first for 10 minutes per side. Blend chipotle peppers with mayonnaise and wine vinegar in the blender. Dice the baked chicken into cubes or small chunks.
2. Mix the chipotle mixture with all the ingredients except tortillas and spinach. Spread 2 oz. of spinach over the tortilla and scoop the stuffing on top. Wrap the tortilla and cut it in half. Serve.

Nutrition: Calories: 300 kcal; **Fat:** 16.4 g; **Carbs:** 8.7 g; **Protein:** 38.5 g

Rosemary Roasted Chicken

Preparation Time: 15 minutes
Cooking Time: 20 minutes
Servings: 8
Ingredients:
- 8 rosemary springs
- Black pepper
- 1 tbsp rosemary, chopped
- 1 chicken
- 1 tbsp organic olive oil

Directions:
1. In a bowl, mix rosemary, rub the chicken with black pepper, the oil, and rosemary mix, place it inside a roasting pan, introduce it inside the oven at 350°F, and roast for sixty minutes and 20 min. Carve chicken, divide between plates and serve using a side dish. Enjoy!

Nutrition: Calories: 325 kcal; **Fat:** 5 g; **Carbs:** 15 g; **Protein:** 14 g

Artichoke and Spinach Chicken

Preparation Time: 15 minutes
Cooking Time: 5 minutes
Servings: 4
Ingredients:
- 10 oz. baby spinach
- ½ tsp red pepper flakes, crushed
- 14 oz. artichoke hearts, chopped
- 28 oz. no-salt-added sauce
- 2 tbsp Essential olive oil
- 4 chicken breasts, boneless and skinless

Directions:
1. Heat up a pan with the oil over medium-high heat, add chicken and red pepper flakes and cook for 5 minutes on them. Add spinach, artichokes, and sauce, toss, cook

for ten minutes more, divide between plates and serve. Enjoy!

Nutrition: Calories: 212 kcal; **Fat:** 3 g; **Carbs:** 16 g; **Protein:** 20 g

Thai Chicken Thighs

Preparation Time: 15 minutes
Cooking Time: 1 hour and 5 minutes
Servings: 6
Ingredients:
- ½ cup Thai sauce
- 4 lb. chicken thighs

Directions:
1. Heat a pan over medium-high heat. Add chicken thighs, brown them for 5 minutes on both sides Transfer to some baking dish, then toss.
2. Introduce within the oven and bake at 400°F for 60 minutes. Divide everything between plates and serve. Enjoy!

Nutrition: Calories: 220 kcal; **Fat:** 4 g; **Carbs:** 12 g; **Protein:** 10 g

Oregano Chicken Thighs

Preparation Time: 15 minutes
Cooking Time: 20 minutes
Servings: 6
Ingredients:
- 12 chicken thighs
- 1 tsp parsley, dried
- ¼ tsp pepper and salt
- ½ cup extra virgin essential olive oil
- 1 cup oregano, chopped
- ¼ cup low-sodium veggie stock

Directions:
1. In your food processor, mix parsley with oregano, salt, pepper, and stock and pulse. Put chicken thighs within the bowl, add oregano paste, toss, cover, and then leave aside within the fridge for 10 minutes.
2. Heat the kitchen grill over medium heat, add chicken pieces, close the lid and cook for twenty or so minutes with them. Divide between plates and serve!

Nutrition: Calories: 254 kcal; **Fat:** 3 g; **Carbs:** 7 g; **Protein:** 17 g

Fish and Seafood

Salmon mushrooms and lentils

Preparation time: 10 minutes
Cooking time: 25 minutes
Servings: 4
INGREDIENTS

- 8 oz. Button mushrooms, sliced
- 8 oz. Salmon steak, cut into slice
- 4 zucchini
- 1 cup red lentils cooked
- 4-6 lettuce leaves
- Sesame seeds
- Salt

DIRECTIONS

1. Cook salmon and mushrooms in pan.
2. Transfer cooked salmon and mushrooms in plate.
3. Arrange veggies and lentils in platter.
4. Drizzle salt, pepper and sesame seeds on top.
5. Serve and enjoy!

NUTRITION:283"calories", "protein"26 g, "carbohydrate" 28 g, "fats" 8 g

Grilled Salmon with Edamame Beans

Preparation Time: 10 minutes
Cooking Time: 14 minutes
Servings: 3
INGREDIENTS:

- 1-pound salmon fillet
- ½ teaspoon thyme
- ½ teaspoon ground coriander

- 1 tablespoon olive oil
- ¼ cup edamame beans, boiled
- 1 tablespoon mustard

DIRECTION:

1. Make a horizontal cut in the salmon and fill it with edamame beans.
2. Then secure the cut with toothpicks.
3. After this, gently rub the fish with thyme, ground coriander, olive oil, and mustard.
4. Preheat the grill to 390F.
5. Put the fish in the preheated grill and cook it for 7 minutes per side.

NUTRITION: Calories: 215; Protein: 12.3g; Carbs: 33.4g; Fat: 19.3g

Salmon with veggies

Preparation time: 10 minutes
Cooking time:20 minutes
Servings: 2
INGREDIENTS

- 1 salmon steak cut into cubes.
- 1 tbsp. Black pepper
- ½ tsp salt
- 2-4 zucchini, sliced
- 4-5 lettuce leaves
- 1 tsp. Sesame seeds

DIRECTIONS

1. Heat the non-stick pan over medium heat and grease with cooking spray.
2. Once the pan is hot, add salmon and cook for 4-5 minutes. Until cooked.
3. Arrange vegetables in a serving bowl and top with salmon bites.
4. Season with salt and pepper, and mix well.
5. Drizzle lime juice, olive oil and sesame seeds on top.
6. Serve and enjoy!

NUTRITION:328"calories", "protein"47 g, "carbohydrate" 9 g, "fats" 11 g,

Fresh Tuna Steak and Fennel Salad

Preparation Time: 15 minutes
Cooking Time: 25 minutes
Servings: 2
Ingredients:
- 2 (1 inch) tuna steaks
- 2 tbsp olive oil, 1 tbsp olive oil for brushing
- 1 tsp black peppercorns, crushed
- 1 tsp fennel seeds, crushed
- 1 fennel bulb, trimmed and sliced
- ½ cup water
- 1 tsp fresh parsley, chopped

Directions:
1. Coat the fish with oil and then season with peppercorns and fennel seeds.
2. Heat the oil on medium heat and sauté the fennel bulb slices for 5 minutes or until light brown.
3. Add the water to the pan and cook for 10 minutes until the fennel is tender.
4. Lower the heat to a simmer.
5. Meanwhile, heat another skillet and sauté the tuna steaks for about 2 to 3 minutes on each side for medium-rare. (Add 1 minute each side for medium and 2 minutes each side for medium well).
6. Serve the fennel mix with the tuna steaks on top and garnish with fresh parsley.

Nutrition: Calories: 288 kcal; **Protein:** 44 g; **Carbohydrates:** 6 g; **Fat:** 9 g

Pan-Seared Haddock with Beets

Preparation Time: 20 minutes
Cooking Time: 30 minutes
Servings: 4

Ingredients:
- 8 beets, peeled and cut into eighths
- 2 shallots, thinly sliced
- 2 tbsp olive oil, divided
- 2 tbsp apple cider vinegar
- 1 tsp fresh thyme, chopped
- Pinch sea salt
- 4 (5 oz./142 g) haddock fillets, patted dry

Directions:
1. Preheat the oven to 400°F (205°C).
5. In a medium bowl, toss together the beets, shallots, and 1 tbsp of olive oil until well coated. Spread the beet mixture in a 9-by-13-inch baking dish. Roast for about 30 minutes, or until the vegetables are caramelized and tender.
6. Remove the beets from the oven and stir in the cider vinegar, thyme, and sea salt.
7. While the beets are roasting, place a large skillet over medium-high heat and add the remaining 1 tbsp of olive oil.
8. Panfry the fish for about 15 minutes, turning once, until it flakes when pressed with a fork. Serve the fish with a generous scoop of roasted beets.

Storage: Store in an airtight container in the fridge for up to 4 days or in the freezer for up to 1 month.

Reheat: Microwave covered, until the desired temperature is reached.

Nutrition: Calories: 314 kcal; **Protein:** 28 g; **Carbohydrates:** 21 g; **Fat:** 9 g

Shrimp Mushroom Squash

Preparation Time: 10 minutes
Cooking Time: 20 minutes
Servings: 4
Ingredients:
- 2 tbsp hemp seeds
- 2 tbsp olive oil
- 1 lb. shrimp, peeled and deveined
- ¼ cup coconut aminos
- 2 tbsp raw honey
- 2 tsp sesame oil
- 4 oz. shiitake mushrooms, (cut into slices)
- 1 red bell pepper, (cut into slices)
- 1 yellow squash, peeled and cubed
- 2 cups chard, chopped

Directions:
1. In a bowl (medium size), mix the aminos, honey, sesame oil, and hemp seeds.
2. In a skillet (you can also use a saucepan); heat the oil over the medium stove flame.
3. Stir the mixture and cook while stirring for about 2−3 minutes until softened.

4. Add the bell pepper, squash, and mushrooms, and stir-cook for 5 minutes.
5. Add the shrimp and aminos mix; stir-cook for 4 minutes more.
6. Add the chard, toss; add into serving bowls and serve.

Nutrition: Calories: 236 kcal; **Protein:** 9 g; **Carbohydrates:** 11 g; **Fat:** 8 g

Spinach Sea Bass Lunch

Preparation Time: 10 minutes
Cooking Time: 30 minutes
Servings: 2
Ingredients:
- 2 sea bass fillets, boneless
- 2 shallots, chopped
- 5 zucchini, halved
- 1 tbsp parsley, chopped
- 1 tbsp olive oil
- 8 oz. baby spinach

Directions:
1. Preheat an oven to 450°F. Grease a baking dish with cooking spray.
2. Add the fish, zucchini, and parsley.
3. Cover the dish and bake for 12–15 minutes and add to serving plates.
4. In a skillet (you can also use a saucepan); heat the oil over the medium stove flame.
5. Add the shallots, stir the mixture and cook while stirring for about 1–2 minutes until softened.
6. Add the spinach, stir, and cook for 4–5 minutes more. Add with the fish and serve warm.

Nutrition: Calories: 218 kcal; **Protein:** 18 g; **Carbohydrates:** 10 g **Fat:** 11 g

Fish Taco Salad with Strawberry Avocado Salsa

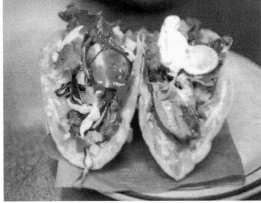

Preparation Time: 20 minutes
Cooking Time: 10 minutes
Servings: 2

Ingredients:
For the salsa:
- 2 hulled and diced strawberries
- ½ small shallot, diced
- 2 tbsp fresh cilantro, finely chopped
- 2 tbsp lime juice, freshly squeezed
- ½ avocado, diced
- 2 tbsp canned black beans, rinsed and drained
- ½ tsp ginger, finely chopped, peeled
- A quarter tsp sea salt

For the fish:
- 1 tsp agave nectar
- 1 cups arugula
- 1 tbsp extra-virgin olive oil or avocado oil
- ½ tbsp lime juice, freshly squeezed
- 1 lb. of light fish (halibut, cod, or red snapper), cut into 2 fillets
- A quarter tsp black pepper, freshly ground
- ½ tsp sea salt

Directions:
1. Preheat the grill, whether it's gas or charcoal.
2. To create the salsa, add the avocado, beans, strawberries, shallot, cilantro, salt, ginger, and lime juice in a medium mixing cup. Put aside after mixing until all of the components are well combined.
3. To render the salad, whisk together the agave, oil, and lime juice in a small bowl. Toss the arugula with the vinaigrette in a big mixing bowl.
4. Season the fish fillets with pepper and salt. Grill the fish for around 7 to 9 minutes over direct high heat, flipping once during cooking. The fish should be translucent and quickly flake.
5. Place one cup of arugula salad on each plate to eat. Cover each salad with a fillet and a heaping spoonful of salsa.

Nutrition: Calories: 878 kcal; **Protein:** 26 g; **Carbohydrates:** 53 g; **Fat:** 26 g

Cod Meal

Preparation Time: 5 minutes
Cooking Time: 35 minutes
Servings: 4
Ingredients:
- 2 tbsp olive oil
- 2 tbsp tarragon, chopped
- ¼ cup parsley, chopped
- 4 cod fillets, skinless
- Black pepper and salt, ground, to the taste
- 1 tbsp thyme, chopped

- 4 cups water

Directions:
1. In a skillet (you can also use a saucepan); heat the oil over the medium stove flame.
2. Stir the mixture, and cook while stirring for about 2–3 minutes until softened.
3. Add the salt, pepper, tarragon, parsley, thyme, water.
4. Boil the mix; add the cod, cook for 12–15 minutes, and drain the liquid.
5. Serve with a side salad.

Nutrition: Calories: 181 kcal; **Protein:** 12 g; **Carbohydrates:** 9 g; **Fat:** 3 g

Halibut in Parchment with Zucchini, Shallots, and Herbs

Preparation Time: 15 minutes
Cooking Time: 15 minutes
Servings: 4
Ingredients:
- ½ cup zucchini, diced small
- 1 shallot, minced
- 4 (5 oz.) halibut fillets (about 1 inch thick)
- 4 tsp extra-virgin olive oil
- ¼ tsp kosher salt
- ⅛ tsp black pepper, freshly ground
- 8 sprigs thyme

Directions:
1. Preheat the oven to 450°F. Combine the zucchini and shallots in a medium bowl. Cut 4 (15-by-24-inch) pieces of parchment paper. Fold each sheet in half horizontally.
2. Draw a large half heart on one side of each folded sheet, with the fold along the heart center. Cut out the heart, open the parchment, and lay it flat.
3. Place a fillet near the center of each parchment heart. Drizzle 1 tsp olive oil on each fillet. Sprinkle with salt and pepper. Top each fillet with 2 sprigs of thyme. Sprinkle each fillet with one-quarter of the zucchini and shallot mixture. Fold the parchment over.
4. Starting at the top, fold the parchment edges over, and continue all the way around to make a packet. Twist the end tightly to secure. Arrange the 4 packets on a baking sheet. Bake for about 15 minutes. Place on plates; cut open. Serve immediately.

Nutrition: Calories: 190 kcal; **Protein:** 20 g; **Carbohydrates:** 5 g; **Fat:** 7 g

Grilled Mahi-Mahi with Artichoke Caponata

Preparation Time: 15 minutes
Cooking Time: 30 minutes
Servings: 4
Ingredients:
- 2 tbsp extra-virgin olive oil
- 2 celery stalks, diced
- ½ cup zucchini, chopped
- ¼ cup white wine
- 2 tbsp white wine vinegar
- 1 can artichoke hearts, drained and chopped
- ¼ cup green olives, pitted and chopped
- 1 tbsp capers, chopped
- ¼ tsp red pepper flakes
- 2 tbsp fresh basil, chopped
- 4 (5 to 6 oz. each) skinless mahi-mahi fillets
- ½ tsp kosher salt
- ¼ tsp black pepper, freshly ground
- Olive oil cooking spray

Directions:
1. Warm-up olive oil in a skillet over medium heat, then put the celery, and sauté for 4 to 5 minutes. Sauté for 30 seconds. Add the zucchini and cook within 2 to 3 minutes. Add the wine and vinegar to deglaze the pan, increasing the heat to medium-high.
2. Add the artichokes, olives, capers, and red pepper flakes and simmer, reducing the liquid by half, for about 10 minutes. Mix in the basil.
3. Season the mahi-mahi with salt and pepper. Heat a grill skillet or grill pan over medium-high heat and coat with olive oil cooking spray. Add the fish and cook within 4 to 5 minutes per side. Serve topped with the artichoke caponata.

Nutrition: Calories: 245 kcal; **Protein:** 24 g; **Carbohydrates:** 10 g; **Fat:** 8 g

Flounder with Zucchini and Basil

Preparation Time: 15 minutes
Cooking Time: 20 minutes
Servings: 4
Ingredients:
- 1 lb. zucchini
- 2 tbsp extra-virgin olive oil
- 2 tbsp basil, cut into ribbons
- ½ tsp kosher salt
- ¼ tsp black pepper, freshly ground

- 4 (5 to 6 oz.) flounder fillets

Directions:
1. Preheat the oven to 425°F.
2. Mix the zucchini, olive oil, basil, salt, and black pepper in a baking dish. Bake for 5 minutes.
3. Remove, then arrange the flounder on top of the zucchini mixture. Bake until the fish is cooked and begins to flake, around 10 to 15 minutes, depending on thickness.

Nutrition: Calories: 215 kcal; **Protein:** 22 g; **Carbohydrates:** 6 g; **Fat:** 9 g

Cod and Cauliflower Chowder

Preparation Time: 15 minutes
Cooking Time: 40 minutes
Servings: 4
Ingredients:
- 2 tbsp extra-virgin olive oil
- 1 leek, sliced thinly
- 1 medium head cauliflower, coarsely chopped
- 1 tsp kosher salt
- ¼ tsp black pepper, freshly ground
- 2 pints zucchini
- 2 cups no-salt-added vegetable stock
- ¼ cup green olives, pitted and chopped
- 1 to 1½ lb. cod
- ¼ cup fresh parsley, minced

Directions:
1. Heat the olive oil in a Dutch oven or large pot over medium heat. Add the leek and sauté until lightly golden brown, about 5 minutes.
2. Sauté within 30 seconds. Add the cauliflower, salt, and black pepper and sauté for 2 to 3 minutes.
3. Add the zucchini and vegetable stock, increase the heat to high and boil, then turn the heat to low and simmer within 10 minutes.
4. Add the olives and mix. Add the fish, cover, and simmer for 20 minutes or until the fish is opaque and flakes easily. Gently mix in the parsley.

Nutrition: Calories: 270 kcal; **Protein:** 18 g; **Carbohydrates:** 19 g; **Fat:** 10 g

Buttered Tuna Lettuce Wraps

Preparation Time: 10 minutes
Cooking Time: 0 minutes
Servings: 2
Ingredients:
- 1 cup almond butter
- 1 tsp low-sodium soy sauce
- ½ tsp sriracha, or to taste
- ½ cup water chestnuts, canned, drained, and chopped
- 2 (2.6 oz. / 74 g) packages tuna, packed in water, drained
- 2 large butter lettuce leaves

Directions:
1. Stir together the almond butter, soy sauce, and sriracha in a medium bowl until well mixed. Add the water chestnuts and tuna and stir until well incorporated.
2. Place 2 butter lettuce leaves on a flat work surface, spoon half of the tuna mixture onto each leaf and roll up into a wrap. Serve immediately.

Nutrition: Calories: 270 kcal; **Protein:** 19 g; **Carbohydrates:** 18 g; **Fat:** 13 g

Tilapia with Limey Cilantro Salsa

Preparation Time: 5 minutes
Cooking Time: 10 minutes
Servings: 2
Ingredients:
Salsa:
- 1 cup mango, chopped
- 2 tbsp fresh cilantro, chopped
- 2 tbsp lime juice, freshly squeezed
- ½ jalapeño pepper, seeded and minced
- Pinch salt

Tilapia:
- 1 tbsp paprika
- ½ tsp thyme, dried
- ½ tsp black pepper, freshly ground
- ¼ tsp salt

- 1 lb. tilapia fillets, boneless
- 2 tsp extra-virgin olive oil
- 1 lime, cut into wedges, for serving

Directions:
1. **Make the salsa:** Place the mango, cilantro, lime juice, jalapeño, and salt in a medium bowl and toss to combine. Set aside.
2. **Make the tilapia:** Stir together the paprika, thyme, black pepper, pepper, and salt in a mini bowl until well mixed. Rub both sides of the fillets generously with the mixture.
3. Heat the olive oil in a huge skillet over medium heat.
4. Add the fish fillets and cook each side for 3 to 5 minutes until golden brown and cooked through.
5. Divide the fillets among 2 plates and spoon half of the prepared salsa onto each fillet. Serve the fish alongside the lime wedges.

Nutrition: Calories: 239 kcal; **Protein:** 25 g; **Carbohydrates:** 21 g; **Fat:** 7.8 g

Peppered Paprika with Grilled Sea Bass

Preparation Time: 20 minutes
Cooking Time: 20 minutes
Servings: 6
Ingredients:
- ¼ tsp paprika
- Sea salt, to taste
- 2 lb. (90 g) sea bass
- 3 tbsp extra-virgin olive oil, divided
- 1 tbsp Italian flat leaf parsley, chopped

Directions:
1. Preheat the grill to high heat.
2. Place the paprika, and sea salt in a large bowl and stir to combine.
3. Dredge the fish in the spice mixture, turning until well coated.
4. Heat 2 tbsp of olive oil in a small skillet. Add the parsley and cook for 1 to 2 minutes, stirring occasionally. Remove the skillet from the heat and set it aside.
5. Brush the grill grates lightly with the remaining 1 tbsp olive oil.
6. Grill the fish for about 7 minutes. Flip the fish and cook for an additional 7 minutes, or until the fish flakes when pressed lightly with a fork.
7. Serve hot.

Nutrition: Calories: 200 kcal; **Protein:** 26 g; **Carbohydrates:** 0.6 g; **Fat:** 10.3 g

Pepper-Infused Tuna Steaks

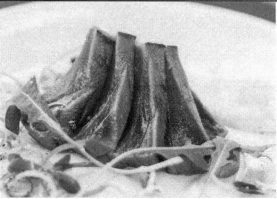

Preparation Time: 5 minutes
Cooking Time: 10 minutes
Servings: 2
Ingredients:
- 2 tuna steaks
- 1 tsp kosher salt
- 2 tbsp olive oil
- 1 tsp whole peppercorns

Directions:
1. On a plate, Season the tuna steaks on both sides with salt.
2. In your skillet, heat the olive oil over medium-high heat until it shimmers.
3. Add the peppercorns and cook for about 5 minutes, or until they soften and pop.
4. Carefully put the tuna steaks in the skillet and sear for 1 to 2 minutes per side, depending on the breadth of the tuna steaks, or until the fish is cooked to the desired level of doneness.
5. Cool for 5 minutes before serving.

Nutrition: Calories: 260 kcal; **Protein:** 33 g; **Carbohydrates:** 0.2 g; **Fat:** 14 g

Sardine Bruschetta with Fennel

Preparation Time: 15 minutes
Cooking Time: 0 minutes
Servings: 4
Ingredients:
- ¼ cup low-fat Greek yogurt
- ½ tbsp light mayonnaise
- ¾ tsp kosher salt, divided
- 1 fennel bulb, cored and thinly sliced
- ¼ cup parsley, chopped, plus more for garnish
- ¼ cup fresh mint, chopped2 tsp extra-virgin olive oil
- ⅛ tsp black pepper, freshly ground
- 8 slices multigrain bread, toasted
- 2 (4.4 oz.) cans sardines, smoked

Directions:

1. Mix the yogurt, mayonnaise, and ¼ tsp of salt in a small bowl.
2. Mix the remaining ½ tsp salt, the fennel, parsley, mint, olive oil, and black pepper in a separate small bowl.
3. Spoon 1 tbsp of the yogurt mixture on each piece of toast. Divide the fennel mixture evenly on top of the yogurt mixture. Divide the sardines among the toasts, placing them on top of the fennel mixture. Garnish with more herbs, if desired.

Nutrition: Calories: 400 kcal; **Protein:** 16 g; **Carbohydrates:** 51 g; **Fat:** 12 g

Chopped Tuna Salad

Preparation Time: 15 minutes
Cooking Time: 0 minutes
Servings: 4
Ingredients:

- 2 tbsp extra-virgin olive oil
- 2 tsp Dijon mustard
- ½ tsp kosher salt
- ¼ tsp black pepper, freshly ground
- 12 olives, pitted and chopped
- ½ cup celery, diced
- ½ cup red bell pepper, diced
- ½ cup fresh parsley, chopped
- 2 (6 oz.) cans no-salt-added tuna, packed in water, drained
- 6 cups baby spinach

Directions:

1. Mix the olive oil, mustard, salt, and black pepper in a medium bowl.
2. Add in the olives, celery, bell pepper, and parsley, and mix well. Add the tuna and gently incorporate.
3. Divide the spinach evenly among 4 plates or bowls. Spoon the tuna salad evenly on top of the spinach.

Nutrition: Calories: 220 kcal; **Protein:** 25 g; **Carbohydrates:** 7 g; **Fat:** 11 g

Monkfish with Sautéed Leeks, Fennel, and Zucchini

Preparation Time: 15 minutes
Cooking Time: 35 minutes
Servings: 4
Ingredients:

- 1 to 1½ lb. monkfish
- 1 tsp kosher salt, divided
- ⅛ tsp black pepper, freshly ground
- 2 tbsp extra-virgin olive oil
- 1 leek, sliced in half lengthwise and thinly sliced
- 2 bulbs fennel, cored and thinly sliced, plus ¼ cup fronds for garnish
- 1 (14.5 oz.) can no-salt-added diced zucchini
- 2 tbsp fresh parsley, chopped
- 2 tbsp fresh oregano, chopped
- ¼ tsp red pepper flakes

Directions:

1. Place the fish in a medium baking dish and add ¼ tsp of salt, plus black pepper. Place in the refrigerator.
2. Warm-up olive oil in a large skillet over medium heat, then put the leek and sauté until translucent, about 3 minutes. Sauté within 30 seconds. Add the fennel and sauté for 4 to 5 minutes. Add the zucchini and simmer for 2 to 3 minutes.
3. Stir in the parsley, oregano, red pepper flakes, the remaining ¾ tsp salt. Put the fish over the leek mixture, cover, and simmer for 20 to 25 minutes. Garnish with the fennel fronds.

Nutrition: Calories: 220 kcal; **Protein:** 22 g; **Carbohydrates:** 11 g; **Fat:** 9 g

Caramelized Fennel and Sardines with Penne

Preparation Time: 15 minutes
Cooking Time: 30 minutes
Servings: 4
Ingredients:

- 8 oz. whole-wheat penne
- 2 tbsp extra-virgin olive oil
- 1 bulb fennel, cored and thinly sliced, plus ¼ cup fronds
- 2 celery stalks, thinly sliced, plus ½ cup leaves
- ¾ tsp kosher salt
- ¼ tsp black pepper, freshly ground

- 2 (4.4 oz.) cans sardines, boneless/skinless, packed in olive oil, undrained

Directions:

1. Cook the penne, as stated in the package directions. Drain, reserving 1 cup of pasta water. Warm-up olive oil in a large skillet over medium heat, then put the fennel and celery and cook within 10 to 12 minutes. Cook within 1 minute.
2. Add the penne, reserved pasta water, salt, and black pepper. Adjust the heat to medium-high and cook for 1 to 2 minutes.
3. Remove, then stir in the fennel fronds, and celery leaves. Break the sardines into bite-size pieces and gently mix them in, along with the oil they were packed in.

Nutrition: Calories: 400 kcal; **Protein:** 22 g; **Carbohydrates:** 46 g; **Fat:** 15 g

Greek Baked Cod

Preparation Time: 9 minutes
Cooking Time: 13 minutes
Servings: 4
Ingredients:

- 1 ½ lb. Cod fillet pieces (4–6 pieces)
- ¼ cup fresh parsley leaves, chopped

For coating:

- ⅓ cup all-purpose flour
- 1 tsp coriander, ground
- ¾ tsp sweet Spanish paprika
- ¾ tsp cumin, ground
- ¾ tsp salt
- ½ tsp black pepper

Directions:

1. Preheat the oven to 400°F.
2. Scourge olive oil, and melted butter, set aside.
3. In another shallow bowl, mix all-purpose flour, spices, salt, and pepper.
4. Pat the fish fillet dry, then dip the fish in the flour mixture, and brush off extra flour.
5. In a cast-iron skillet over medium-high heat, add 2 tbsp olive oil.
6. Once heated, add in the fish and sear on each side for color, but do not thoroughly cook, remove from heat.
7. Drizzle all over the fish fillets.
8. Bake for 10 minutes, until it begins to flake easily with a fork.
9. Allow the dish to cool completely.
10. Distribute among the containers, and store for 2–3 days.

11. To Serve: Reheat in the microwave for 1–2 minutes or until heated through. Sprinkle chopped parsley. Enjoy!

Nutrition: Calories: 321 kcal; **Protein:** 23 g; **Carbohydrates:** 14 g; **Fat:** 13 g

Green Goddess Crab Salad with Endive

Preparation Time: 15 minutes
Cooking Time: 10 minutes
Servings: 4
Ingredients:

- 1 lb. lump crabmeat
- ⅔ cup low-fat Greek yogurt
- 3 tbsp mayonnaise
- 3 tbsp fresh chives, chopped, plus additional for garnish
- 3 tbsp fresh parsley, chopped, plus extra for garnish
- 3 tbsp fresh basil, chopped, plus extra for garnish
- ½ tsp kosher salt
- ¼ tsp black pepper, freshly ground
- 4 endives, ends cut off, and leaves separated

Directions:

1. In a medium bowl, combine the crab, yogurt, mayonnaise, chives, parsley, basil, salt, plus black pepper, and mix until well combined.
2. Place the endive leaves on 4 salad plates. Divide the crab mixture evenly on top of the endive. Garnish with additional herbs, if desired.

Nutrition: Calories: 200 kcal; **Protein:** 25 g; **Carbohydrates:** 44 g; **Fat:** 7 g

Seared Scallops with Blood Orange Glaze

Preparation Time: 15 minutes
Cooking Time: 20 minutes
Servings: 4
Ingredients:

- 3 tbsp extra-virgin olive oil, divided
- ½ tsp kosher salt, divided
- 4 blood oranges, juiced
- 1 tsp blood orange zest
- ½ tsp red pepper flakes
- 1 lb. scallops, small side muscle removed
- ¼ tsp black pepper, freshly ground
- ¼ cup fresh chives, chopped

Directions:

1. Heat 1 tbsp of the olive oil in a small saucepan over medium-high heat. Add ¼ tsp of the salt and sauté for 30 seconds.
2. Add the orange juice and zest, bring to a boil, reduce the heat to medium-low, and cook within 20 minutes, or until the liquid reduces by half and becomes a thicker syrup consistency. Remove and mix in the red pepper flakes.
3. Pat the scallops dry with a paper towel and season with the remaining ¼ tsp salt and the black pepper. Heat the remaining 2 tbsp of olive oil in a large skillet on medium-high heat. Add the scallops gently and sear.
4. Cook on each side within 2 minutes. If cooking in 2 batches, use 1 tbsp of oil per batch. Serve the scallops with the blood orange glaze and garnish with the chives.

Nutrition: Calories: 140 kcal; **Protein:** 15 g; **Carbohydrates:** 12 g; **Fat:** 4 g

Shrimp

Preparation Time: 15 minutes
Cooking Time: 10 minutes
Servings: 4
Ingredients:
- 2 tbsp extra-virgin olive oil
- ½ tsp kosher salt
- ¼ tsp red pepper flakes
- 1 lb. large shrimp, peeled and deveined
- ½ cup white wine
- 3 tbsp fresh parsley, minced

Directions:
1. Heat the olive oil in a wok or large skillet over medium-high heat. Add salt, and red pepper flakes and sauté, 30 seconds to 1 minute.
2. Add the shrimp and cook within 2 to 3 minutes on each side. Pour in the wine and deglaze the wok, scraping up any flavorful brown bits, for 1 to 2 minutes. Turn off the heat; mix in the parsley.

Nutrition: Calories: 200 kcal; **Protein:** 23 g; **Carbohydrates:** 3 g; **Fat:** 9 g

Tuna With Vegetable Mix

Preparation Time: 8 minutes
Cooking Time: 16 minutes
Servings: 4
Ingredients:
- 2 tbsp extra-virgin olive oil divided
- 1 tbsp rice vinegar
- 1 tsp kosher salt, divided
- ¾ tsp Dijon mustard
- ¾ tsp honey
- 4 oz. baby gold beets, thinly sliced
- 4 oz. fennel bulb, trimmed and thinly sliced
- 4 oz. baby turnips, thinly sliced
- 6 oz. Granny Smith apple, very thinly sliced
- 2 tsp sesame seeds, toasted
- 6 oz. tuna steaks
- ½ tsp black pepper
- 1 tbsp fennel fronds, torn

Directions:
1. Scourge 2 tbsp of oil, ½ a tsp of salt, honey, vinegar, and mustard.
2. Give the mixture a nice mix.
3. Add fennel, beets, apple, and turnips; mix and toss until everything is evenly coated.
4. Sprinkle with sesame seeds and toss well.
5. Using a cast-iron skillet, heat 2 tbsp of oil over high heat.
6. Carefully season the tuna with ½ a tsp of salt and pepper
7. Situate the tuna in the skillet and cook for 4 minutes, giving 1½ minutes per side.
8. Remove the tuna and slice it up.
9. Place in containers with the vegetable mix.
10. Serve with the fennel mix, and enjoy!

Nutrition: Calories: 443 kcal; **Protein:** 19.5 g; **Carbohydrates:** 19 g; **Fat:** 13.1 g

Fish Kebab Skewers

Preparation time: 15 minutes
Cooking time: 15 minutes

Servings:4
Ingredients

- 1 lb. ground salmon
- 1/4 cup chopped fresh parsley
- 1/4 tsp. ground coriander
- 1/4 tsp. ground paprika
- 2 eggs

Directions

1. Preheat grill over medium heat and grease it with cooking spray.
2. Mix all recipe kebab ingredients in a bowl.
3. Thread the mixture over 4 wooden skewers and shape them into kebab.
4. Grill Kebab for 4-5 minutes each side, until cooked and golden brown.
5. Enjoy!

Nutrition 278"Calories", "Protein"29 g"Carbohydrate" 3 g, "Fats" 16 g, "Sugar" 1 g

Salmon & Zucchini Skewers

Preparation time: 5 minutes
Cooking time: 15minutes
Servings:4
Ingredients

- 1 salmon fillet, cut into cubes
- 1 zucchini, thinly sliced lengthwise
- Salt and pepper to taste
- 4-5 zucchini for serving
- Parsley leaves for serving

Directions

1. Coat salmon and zucchini with spices and thread on wooden skewers.
2. Grill skewers for about 4-5 minutes per side until cooked and brown.
3. Once cooked remove from grill
4. Serve with fresh veggies.
5. Enjoy.

Nutrition
171"Calories", "Protein"23 g, "Carbohydrate" 7 g, "Fats" 5 g, "Sugar" 3 g

Baked Salmon Loaf

Preparation time: 10 minutes
Cooking time: 40 minutes
Servings:4
Ingredients

- 1 lb. salmon, ground
- 2 large egg
- 2 tbsps. Italian seasoning
- Salt and pepper, to taste
- 1/2 cup green peas

Directions

1. Mix all loaf ingredients in mixing bowl and press it in greased loaf pan evenly.
2. Preheat oven to 325 F.
3. Place loaf pan in preheated oven and bake loaf for about 30-40 minutes in preheated oven
4. Once loaf is cooked remove from oven.
5. Serve with fresh salad and sauce.
6. Enjoy!

Nutrition
211"Calories", "Protein"27 g, "Carbohydrate" 6 g, "Fats" 7 g, "Sugar" 2 g

Salmon & Peas

Preparation time:10 minutes
Cooking time: 20 minutes
Servings:
Ingredients

- 1 salmon fillet cut into cubes
- 1 cup peas
- 1 cup zucchini puree
- salt & pepper to taste
- 1 tsp. paprika powder
- 1 tsp. cumin seeds
- 1 tsp red chilli powder
- 1/2 tsp. turmeric powder
- 1 oz. parsley chopped

Directions

1. Add zucchini in a blender and make a smooth paste.
2. Heat a non-stick pan over medium heat, and cook for 1 minute.
3. Add salmon, peas, seasoning and cook again for 4-5 minutes.
4. Once cooked remove from pan.
5. Enjoy!

Nutrition
386"Calories", "Protein"50 g, "Carbohydrate" 22 g, "Fats" 10 g, "Sugar" 10 g

Creamy Salmon

Preparation time:10 minutes

Cooking time: 20 minutes
Servings:
Ingredients
- 1 salmon fillet cut into bite size
- 1 cup low fat Greek yogurt
- salt & pepper to taste
- 1 tsp. paprika powder
- 1 tsp. cumin seeds
- 2 tbsps. chopped parsley

Directions
1. Heat a non-stick pan over medium heat.
2. Add salmon cubes in pan and cook for 4-5 minutes until salmon is brown.
3. Add Greek yogurt and spices in pan, cook for about 3-4 minutes.
4. Once cooked remove from pan
5. Sprinkle parsley on top.
6. Enjoy.

Nutrition
398"Calories", "Protein"40 g, "Carbohydrate" 12 g, "Fats" 11 g, "Sugar" 5 g

Baked Fish In Herbs

Preparation time: 10 minutes
Cooking time:15 minutes
Servings: 4
Ingredients
1 Whole fish, 2 lb.
- salt & pepper to taste
- 1 tsp. paprika powder
- 1 tsp. cumin seeds
- 4 tbsps. lime juice

Directions
1. Add all ingredients in a bowl and mix well.
2. Arrange fish in greased baking tray and top with spice mix.
3. Bake fish in an oven for about 40 minutes until cooked and brown on top.
4. Enjoy.

Nutrition
309"Calories", "Protein"47 g, "Carbohydrate" 5 g, "Fats" 10 g, "Sugar" 1 g

Grilled Fish With Lime & Parsley

Preparation time: 10 minutes
Cooking time:20 minutes
Servings: 4
Ingredients
2 lb. fish, washed and slits
- salt & pepper to taste

- 1 tsp. paprika powder
- ¼ cup lime juice
- ¼ cup finely chopped parsley

Directions
1. Mix all spices in a bowl and marinate fish in this mixture for about 2 hours.
2. Grill fish in preheated grill for about 8-12 minutes per side until cooked.
3. Sprinkle chopped parsley on top.
4. Enjoy.

Nutrition
299"Calories", "Protein"46 g, "Carbohydrate" 2 g, "Fats" 10 g, "Sugar" 0 g

Salmon With Pesto And Beans

Preparation time: 10 minutes
Cooking time: 15 minutes
Servings:2
Ingredients
2 salmon fillet
- 1 tbsp. Italian seasoning
- Salt and pepper, to taste
- green beans for serving

PESTO SAUCE
- 1 cup basil leaves
- tbsp. lime juice
- pinch salt

Directions
1. Rub salmon fillet with all spices
2. Grill salmon fillet with beans for 4-5 minutes per side.
3. Once cooked remove from grill.
4. Meanwhile, blend pesto ingredients in a blender.
5. Drizzle pesto sauce over the salmon fillet.
6. Serve and enjoy!

Nutrition Facts
439"Calories", "Protein"66 g, "Carbohydrate" 7 g, "Fats" 14 g, "Sugar" 2 g

Baked Fish With Veggies

Preparation time: 10 minutes
Cooking time:20 minutes
Servings: 4
Ingredients
- 1 whole fish, washed and slits
- 1 tbsp. Italian seasoning
- Salt and pepper, to taste
- ¼ cup lime juice

- 1 eggplant sliced
- 1 zucchini, sliced
- 1 yellow bell pepper, sliced
- parsley & lettuce leaves for serving.

Directions

1. Mix all spices in a bowl and rub it over fish and veggies
2. Coat this mixture over vegetables and fish and marinate for 1 hour.
3. Bake fish in veggies in preheated oven for about 20-25 minutes until veggies and fish is tender.
4. Serve with fresh veggies.
5. Enjoy!

Nutrition

313"Calories", "Protein"47 g, "Carbohydrate" 5 g, "Fats" 10 g, "Sugar" 2 g

Salmon With Mushrooms

Preparation time: 10 minutes
Cooking time:20 minutes
Servings: 2
Ingredients

- 2 salmon fillet
- 1/2 lb. needle mushrooms
- 2 tbsps. lime juice
- Salt and pepper, to taste

Directions

1. Mix all spices in bowl and rub it over mushrooms and salmon.
2. Grill fillet and mushroom for about4-5 minutes until cooked.

3. Drizzle Lime juice on top.
4. Serve and enjoy!

Nutrition

429"Calories", "Protein"68 g, "Carbohydrate" 3 g, "Fats" 14 g, "Sugar" 2 g

Grilled Salmon With Asparagus

Preparation time: 10 minutes
Cooking time:20 minutes
Servings: 2
Ingredients

- 2 salmon fillet
- 1 lb. baby asparagus, trimmed and peeled
- 2 zucchini
- 1 tbsp. Italian seasoning
- Salt and pepper, to taste
- Lettuce leaves

Directions

1. Rub salmon fillet, asparagus and zucchini with all spices.
2. Place veggies and salmon in electric grill and grill for about 5-8 minutes per side.
3. Drizzle pepper on top.
4. Serve and enjoy!

Nutrition

451"Calories", "Protein"70 g, "Carbohydrate" 9 g, "Fats" 14 g, "Sugar" 4 g

Soup and Stews

Chicken Soup

Preparation Time: 10 minutes
Cooking Time: 20 minutes
Servings: 4
Ingredients:

- 10 cups chicken broth
- 2 lb. chicken
- Salt and pepper

Directions:

1. Add all ingredients to the cooking pan.
2. Bring mixture to boil and simmer on low heat for about 20–25 minutes until chicken is cooked.
3. Sprinkle lime juice on top.
4. Serve immediately.
5. Enjoy!

Nutrition: Calories: 267 kcal; **Protein:** 50 g; **Carbohydrates:** 4 g; **Fat:** 3 g

Cauliflower and Broccoli Soup

Preparation Time: 10 minutes
Cooking Time: 20 minutes
Servings: 4
Ingredients:

- 1 medium broccoli florets
- 1 medium, cauliflower
- 4 cups chicken stock
- 1 tsp salt
- 1 tsp pepper
- 1 tbsp parsley chopped

Directions:

1. Heat a pan over medium heat.
2. Once the pan is hot, cook broccoli and cauliflower for about 4–5 minutes.
3. Add broth and cook on low heat for 15–20 minutes.
4. Add in salt, pepper, and parsley.

5. Serve hot and enjoy!
Nutrition: Calories: 68 kcal; **Protein:** 4 g; **Carbohydrates:** 11 g; **Fat:** 1 g

Salmon and Potato Soup with Herbs

Preparation Time: 10 minutes
Cooking Time: 15 minutes
Servings: 4
Ingredients:

- 1 lb. salmon fillet cut into cubes
- 2–3 medium sweet potatoes, cut into cubes
- ¼ tsp black pepper
- ½ tsp salt
- warm water to cover
- 1 tbsp lime juice

Directions:

1. Add all ingredients
2. Add 6 cups of hot water to cover completely.
3. Cook covered for about 30 minutes to simmer on low heat.
4. Once cooked remove from pan.
5. Serve hot and enjoy!

Nutrition: Calories: 223 kcal; **Protein:** 14 g; **Carbohydrates:** 18 g; **Fat:** 5 g

Sweet Corn Soup with Herbs

Preparation Time: 15 minutes
Cooking Time: 20 minutes
Servings: 4
Ingredients:
- 1 can sweet corns, drained
- 6 cups chicken stock
- Salt, to taste
- Pepper, to taste
- 1 tbsp lime juice
- Parsley

Directions:
1. Add all ingredients to the cooking pan.
2. Cover and cook soup on low heat for about 15–20 minutes until soup is cooked.
3. Blend soup in an electric blender for about 5–10 seconds.
4. Pour cooked soup into a serving bowl.
5. Top with some sweet corns and parsley and lime juice.
6. Enjoy!

Nutrition: Calories: 96 kcal; **Protein:** 2 g; **Carbohydrates:** 23 g; **Fat:** 0 g

Kidney Beans and Zucchini Soup

Preparation Time: 10 minutes
Cooking Time: 30 minutes
Servings: 4
Ingredients:
- 1 can kidney beans, drained
- 1 cup zucchini puree
- 6 cups chicken stock
- Salt and pepper, to taste

Directions:
1. Place all ingredients in a pan and cook on low heat for 20 minutes until soup is thick.
2. Taste and add salt, if needed.
3. Enjoy hot!

Nutrition: Calories: 262 kcal; **Protein:** 12 g; **Carbohydrates:** 36 g; **Fat:** 6 g

Traditional Russian Cold Soup

Preparation Time: 10 minutes
Cooking Time: 20 minutes
Servings: 4
Ingredients:
- 1 boiled sweet potato, chopped
- ¼ cup zucchini, chopped
- 1 cup low-fat Greek yogurt
- 1 cucumber, chopped
- 1 oz. rosemary, chopped
- ⅛ tsp black pepper
- ¼ tsp salt

Directions:
1. Add all ingredients to the serving bowl and mix well.
2. Serve and enjoy!

Nutrition: Calories: 113 kcal; **Protein:** 8 g; **Carbohydrates:** 13 g; **Fat:** 1 g

Chicken Soup with Carrots

Preparation Time: 5 minutes
Cooking Time: 25 minutes
Servings: 2
Ingredients:
- 1 chicken breast,
- 1 carrot, sliced
- 4 cups chicken broth
- Salt and pepper to taste
- ¼ cup parsley leaves

Directions:

1. Add all ingredients to the cooking pan and mix well.
2. Cover and cook on low heat for about 25–30 minutes until veggies are cooked.
3. Sprinkle parsley leaves on top.
4. Serve and enjoy hot.

Nutrition: Calories: 291 kcal; **Protein:** 24 g; **Carbohydrates:** 3 g; **Fat:** 6 g

Chicken and Veggies Stew

Preparation Time: 10 minutes
Cooking Time: 20 minutes
Servings: 2
Ingredients:

- ½ lb. chicken, boiled and shredded
- 1 carrot, sliced
- ¼ cup green peas
- 4 cups chicken stock
- ½ tsp salt
- ¼ tsp black pepper
- 1 tbsp lime juice.
- ¼ cup parsley, chopped

Directions:

1. Heat the non-stick soup pot over medium heat.
2. Once the pan is hot, add all ingredients in the pan and cook for about 4–5 minutes.
3. Add the stock and season with salt, and pepper.
4. Cook covered for about 15–20 minutes on low heat until veggies are cooked through.
5. Sprinkle lime juice on top.
6. Adjust seasoning according to taste and enjoy!

Nutrition: Calories: 147 kcal; **Protein:** 14 g; **Carbohydrates:** 3 g; **Fat:** 3 g

Lentils Soup with Herbs

Preparation Time: 10 minutes
Cooking Time: 20 minutes
Servings: 4
Ingredients:

- ¼ cup red lentils, soaked and drained
- 4 cups chicken broth
- salt and pepper, to taste

Topping:

- 1 zucchini, chopped
- Parsley
- 1 tbsp lime juice

Directions:

1. Heat a saucepan over medium heat, and grease with cooking spray.
2. Once the pan is hot, add lentils, and broth, and cook covered for about 15–20 minutes.
3. Season with salt to taste, and mix well.
4. Add the rest of the ingredients and mix well.
5. Serve and enjoy!

Nutrition: Calories: 82 kcal; **Protein:** 4 g; **Carbohydrates:** 17 g; **Fat:** 2 g

Shrimp Soup with Cream

Preparation Time: 10 minutes
Cooking Time: 20 minutes
Servings: 4
Ingredients:

- 1 lb. shrimp,
- 4–5 bay leaves
- 1 zucchini sliced
- 4 cups chicken stock
- 1 cup Greek yogurt
- salt and pepper, to taste

Directions:

1. Heat the saucepan over medium heat and grease it with cooking spray.
2. Once the pan is hot, add shrimp and cook for about another 2–3 minutes.
3. Add the rest of the ingredients and cook on low heat for 4–5 minutes.
4. Pour soup into a serving bowl with fresh veggies.
5. Drizzle lime juice on top.
6. Serve hot.

Nutrition: Calories: 137 kcal; **Protein:** 13 g; **Carbohydrates:** 3 g; **Fat:** 0 g

Mushroom and Chicken Soup

Preparation Time: 10 minutes
Cooking Time: 25 minutes
Servings: 4
Ingredients:

- 1 chicken breast, cut into cubes
- ½ lb. button mushrooms. sliced
- Salt and pepper, to taste
- 6 cups. chicken stock
- 4–5 whole red pepper
- Parsley

Directions:

1. Heat the cooking pan over medium and grease with cooking spray.
2. Cook for about 5–8 minutes until the chicken is no longer pink and the mushrooms are shrinking.
3. Add stock, red pepper, spices, and Greek yogurt and cook covered for about 8–10 minutes.
4. Pour soup into bowls.
5. Serve and enjoy!

Nutrition: Calories: 176 kcal; **Protein:** 22 g; **Carbohydrates:** 7 g; **Fat:** 3 g

Shrimp and Zucchini Stew

Preparation Time: 5 minutes

Cooking Time: 15 minutes
Servings: 2
Ingredients:

- 1 lb. shrimp, peeled
- 1 zucchini, roughly sliced
- 1 bunch kale, trimmed and chopped
- ½ tsp salt and pepper
- 4 cups chicken broth

Directions:

1. Add all ingredients to the cooking pan and cook on medium heat.
2. Bring mixture boil to a simmer for about 5–8 minutes until soup is cooked through.
3. Sprinkle parsley leaves on top.
4. Enjoy!

Nutrition: Calories: 173 kcal; **Protein:** 28 g; **Carbohydrates:** 10 g; **Fat:** 2 g

Beans and Veggies Soup

Preparation Time: 10 minutes
Cooking Time: 25 minutes
Servings: 4
Ingredients:

- 2 cups broccoli, chopped
- 1 carrot, chopped
- 1 cup kidney beans, drained
- 3 cups chicken stock
- ¼ tsp salt
- ⅛ tsp pepper
- 1 tbsp lime juice

Directions:

1. Add all ingredients to the cooking pan and cook on medium heat.
2. Bring mixture boil to a simmer for about 25 minutes until soup is cooked through.
3. Sprinkle parsley leaves on top.

Nutrition: Calories: 105 kcal; **Protein:** 6 g; **Carbohydrates:** 10 g; **Fat:** 4 g

French Lentils Soup

Preparation Time: 10 minutes
Cooking Time: 20 minutes
Servings: 4
Ingredients:

- 1 cup French lentils, soaked and drained
- Salt and pepper
- 6 cups chicken broth
- Salt and peppcr, to taste
- 1 zucchini, chopped
- Parsley, chopped

Directions:

1. Add all ingredients to the cooking pan and cook on medium heat.
2. Bring mixture boil to a simmer for about 20 minutes until soup is cooked through.
3. Sprinkle parsley leaves on top.
4. Enjoy!

Nutrition: Calories: 217 kcal; **Protein:** 13 g; **Carbohydrates:** 41 g; **Fat:** 0 g

Salmon and Corn Soup

Preparation Time: 10 minutes
Cooking Time: 20 minutes
Servings: 4
Ingredients:

- 8 oz. green beans
- 1 carrot, chopped
- 1 lb. chicken, cut into slice
- 1 cup sweet corn, boil

- 4 cups chicken stock
- ½ tsp salt
- ¼ tsp black pepper

Directions:

1. Add all ingredients to the cooking pan and cook on medium heat.
2. Bring mixture boil to a simmer for about 20 minutes until soup is cooked through.
3. Sprinkle parsley leaves on top.
4. Enjoy!

Nutrition: Calories: 192 kcal; **Protein:** 25 g; **Carbohydrates:** 15 g; **Fat:** 3 g

Cabbage Stew

Preparation Time: 10 minutes
Cooking Time: 20 minutes
Servings: 4
Ingredients:

- 1 green cabbage, shredded
- 2 cups cauliflower, roughly chopped
- 1 cup sweet potato, chopped
- 1 cup green peas.
- 4 cups vegetable broth
- Salt and black pepper to taste
- 2 lime juice
- ½ cup parsley, chopped

Directions:

1. Add all ingredients to the cooking pan and cook on medium heat.
2. Bring mixture boil to a simmer for about 20 minutes until soup is cooked through.
3. Sprinkle parsley leaves on top.
4. Enjoy!

Nutrition: Calories: 85 kcal; **Protein:** 4 g; **Carbohydrates:** 17 g; **Fat:** 0 g

Detox instant veggies soup

Preparation time: 5 minutes
Cooking time: 20 minutes
Servings: 1

INGREDIENTS

1. 1 carrot, sliced
2. 8 oz. Green beans
3. 2 cups broccoli, florets
4. 1 cup cauliflower, florets.
5. 1 zucchini, sliced
6. 1 tsp. Cumin seed powder
7. ½ tsp. Sea salt
8. 4 cups water

DIRECTIONS

1. Add all ingredients in cooking pan and cook on medium heat.
2. Bring mixture boil to a simmer for about 20 minutes until soup is cooked through.
3. Sprinkle parsley leaves on top.
4. Enjoy!

NUTRITION: 171 Calories, Protein: 14 g, Carbohydrates: 17 g, Fat: 0 g,

Salads

Buddha lunch bowl

Preparation time: 10 minutes
Cooking time: 10 minutes
Servings: 2
INGREDIENTS

- 4-5 zucchini, sliced
- Salt and pepper to taste
- 1 cucumber sliced
- 4-5 radish, sliced
- 1 can chickpeas, rinsed
- 1 firm ripe avocado, diced
- ¼ cup chopped fresh parsley

DIRECTIONS

1. Cut vegetables and arrange in a bowl.
2. Sprinkle salt and pepper on top.
3. Serve and enjoy!

NUTRITION: 336 "calories", "protein" 12 g, "carbohydrate" 43 g, "fats" 18 g

Greek salad with fresh vegetables

Preparation time: 10 minutes
Cooking time: minutes
Servings: 2
INGREDIENTS

- 1 cucumber sliced
- 5-8 zucchini, half
- 4-5 lettuce leaves, chopped
- 1 cup kidney beans, boil
- 1 cup low fat feta cheese, cubes

Dressing

- ¾ tsp. Salt
- ½ tsp dried thyme
- ½ tsp paprika

DIRECTIONS

1. Mix dressing ingredients in bowl.
2. Add cucumber, zucchini, lettuce leaves, beans, and cheese in serving bowl.
3. Pour dressing over vegetables and mix well.
4. Serve chill and enjoy!

NUTRITION: 327 "calories", "protein" 10 g, "carbohydrate" 23 g, "fats" 20 g

Tuna & veggies salad

Preparation time: 15 minutes
Cooking time: 15 minutes
Servings: 2

INGREDIENTS

- 1 egg, boil cut into halves
- 1 cup tuna, steamed
- 1 avocado sliced.
- 4-5 zucchini, sliced
- 4-5 lettuce leaves, chopped
- 4 oz. Green beans
- Salt and pepper to taste

DIRECTIONS

1. Add veggies, tuna and boiled egg in serving bowl.
2. Drizzle salt and pepper on top and mix it.
3. Serve and enjoy!

NUTRITION: 348 "calories", "protein" 22 g, "carbohydrate" 32 g, "fats" 18 g,

Lettuce & pomegranate salad

Preparation time: 20 minutes
Cooking time: minutes
Servings: 2
INGREDIENTS

- 1 bunch lettuce leaves
- 1 cup pomegranate seeds
- 1 cup baby spinach leaves

DIRECTIONS

1. Cut veggies and arrange in a serving plate.
2. Drizzle lime juice, salt, and pepper on top.
3. Enjoy!

NUTRITION: 75 "calories", "protein" 2 g, "carbohydrate" 13 g, "fats" 0 g,

Falafel fresh salad

Preparation time: 10 minutes
Cooking time: 20 minutes
Servings: 2
INGREDIENTS

- 4 medium zucchini, cut into thick slice
- Salt and pepper to taste
- 2 tortilla
- 4-5 falafel
- Lettuce leaves
- ¼ cup Greek yogurt

DIRECTIONS

1. Toss tortilla on a griddle for about 2-3 minutes.
2. Arrange falafel, zucchini slice, lettuce leaves on tortilla and top with Greek yogurt.
3. Drizzle salt and pepper on top.
4. Serve and enjoy!

NUTRITION: 297"calories", "protein"12 g, "carbohydrate" 40 g, "fats" 9 g,

Tacos with guacamole & chickpeas

Preparation time: 10 minutes
Cooking time: 20 minutes
Servings: 2
INGREDIENTS

- 1 cup guacamole
- 4 zucchini, sliced
- 1 cup chickpeas, boiled
- 12–15 mint leaves, finely chopped
- Arugula leaves
- Salt & pepper
- 3–4 tbsps. Lime juice

DIRECTIONS

1. Spread guacamole in a plate with knife.
2. Arrange zucchini slice, chickpeas and arugula leaves on it.
3. Drizzle lime juice, salt, and pepper on top.
4. Serve and enjoy!

NUTRITION: 429"calories", "protein"15 g, "carbohydrate" 41 g, "fats" 18 g

Cucumber salad

Preparation time: 10 minutes
Cooking time: 20 minutes
Servings: 2
INGREDIENTS

- 2 cucumbers, thinly sliced
- Salt & pepper
- 3–4 tbsps. Lime juice

DIRECTIONS

1. Add cucumber slice in serving plate.
2. Drizzle, lime juice, salt and pepper on top.
3. Serve chill and enjoy it!

NUTRITION: 60"calories", "protein"1 g, "carbohydrate" 13 g, "fats" 0 g

Cobb salad traditional

Preparation time: 20 minutes
Cooking time: 10 minutes
Servings: 4
INGREDIENTS

- 1/3 cup lime juice
- 1 tbsp. Mustard
- Salt & pepper
- 1 bunch romaine lettuce, chopped
- 4 hard-boiled eggs, peeled and quartered
- 12 oz. Boil chicken, diced
- 1 avocado, thinly sliced
- 5 oz. Zucchini, halved

DIRECTIONS

1. Mix lime juice, mustard, salt, and pepper in jar.
2. Arrange vegetables in serving platter and top with dressing ingredients.
3. Season with salt and pepper, drizzle with dressing.
4. Serve and enjoy!

NUTRITION: 380"calories", "protein"30 g, "carbohydrate" 14 g, "fats" 18 g

Buddha bowl with baked potatoes

Preparation time: 10 minutes
Cooking time: 25 minutes
Servings: 4
INGREDIENTS

- 1 cup sweet corn boil
- 5 sweet potatoes, bakes and sliced
- 1 cucumber sliced
- 4-5 zucchini, sliced
- 1 avocado, sliced
- 1 bunch lettuce leaves
- Salt and pepper
- 3–4 tbsps. Lime juice

DIRECTIONS

1. Arrange all cooked veggies in serving platter.
2. Drizzle salt, pepper and lime juice on top.
3. Serve chill.
4. Enjoy!

NUTRITION: 324"calories", "protein"5 g, "carbohydrate" 50 g, "fats" 8 g

Zucchini olives and beans salad

Preparation time: 10 minutes
Cooking time: 25 minutes
Servings: 4
INGREDIENTS

- 1 zucchini, thinly sliced
- 4 oz. Black olives
- 1 cup white beans, cooked

- 1 cup cauliflower, steamed
- Salt and pepper
- 3–4 tbsps. Lime juice

DIRECTIONS

1. Mix all ingredients in serving platter, season with salt and pepper, and mix well.
2. Drizzle lime juice on top.
3. Enjoy!

NUTRITION: 171"calories", "protein"8 g, "carbohydrate" 27 g, "fats" 3 g,

Avocado salad

Preparation time: 10 minutes
Cooking time: minutes
Servings: 2
INGREDIENTS

- 1 avocado, thinly sliced
- 1 bunch lettuce leaves, chopped

DIRECTIONS

1. Add all ingredients in serving plate.
2. Serve and enjoy!

NUTRITION: 165"calories", "protein"2 g, "carbohydrate" 9 g, "fats" 14 g,

Zucchini and Avocado Salad

Preparation Time: 10 minutes
Cooking Time: 0 minutes
Servings: 4
Ingredients:

- 1 lb. zucchini
- 2 avocados
- 1 and ½ tbsp olive oil
- Handful basil, chopped

Directions:

1. Mix the zucchini with the avocados and the rest of the ingredients in a serving bowl, toss and serve right away.

Nutrition: Calories: 148 kcal; **Protein:** 5.5 g; **Carbohydrates:** 9 g; **Fat:** 7.8 g

Beans and Cucumber Salad

Preparation Time: 10 minutes
Cooking Time: 0 minutes
Servings: 4
Ingredients:

- 15 oz. great northern beans. canned
- 2 tbsp olive oil
- ½ cup baby arugula
- 1 cup cucumber
- 1 tbsp parsley
- 2 zucchini, cubed
- 2 tbsp balsamic vinegar

Directions:

1. Mix the beans with the cucumber and the rest of the ingredients in a large bowl, toss and serve cold.

Nutrition: Calories: 233 kcal; **Protein:** 8 g; **Carbohydrates:** 13 g; **Fat:** 9 g

Chickpeas and quinoa salad

Preparation time: 10 minutes
Cooking time: 25 minutes
Servings: 2
INGREDIENTS

- 1 cup chickpeas, boil
- 1 cup quinoa, cooked
- 4-5 zucchini, chopped
- 8 oz. Spinach, chopped
- Salt and pepper
- 3–4 tbsps. Lime juice

DIRECTIONS

1. Add all cooked items and chopped veggies in bowl and mix well.
2. Serve and enjoy!

NUTRITION: 347"calories", "protein"17 g, "carbohydrate" 64 g, "fats" 3 g

Beets and Honey Salad

Preparation time: 10 minutes
Cooking time: 7 hours
Servings: 12
INGREDIENTS:

- 5 beets, peeled and sliced
- ¼ cup balsamic vinegar
- 1/3 cup honey
- 1 tablespoon rosemary, chopped
- 2 tablespoons olive oil

DIRECTIONS:

1. In your Slow cooker, mix beets with vinegar, honey, oil, and rosemary, cover, and cook on Low for 7 hours.
2. Divide between plates and serve as a side dish.

NUTRITION: 70 calories, 0.8g protein, 12.3g carbohydrates, 2.5g fat, 1g fiber, 0mg cholesterol, 33mg sodium, 140mg potassium.

Carrot Side Salad

Preparation time: 10 minutes
Cooking time: 7 hours
Servings: 6
INGREDIENTS:

- ½ cup walnuts, chopped
- 2 tablespoons olive oil
- 1 shallot, chopped

- 1 teaspoon Dijon mustard
- 1 tablespoon honey
- 2 beets, peeled and cut into wedges
- 2 carrots, peeled and sliced
- 1 cup parsley
- 5 ounces arugula

DIRECTIONS:

1. In your Slow cooker, mix beets with carrots, honey, mustard, shallot, oil, and walnuts, cover, and cook on Low for 7 hours.
2. Transfer everything to a bowl, add parsley and arugula, toss, divide between plates and serve as a side dish.

NUTRITION: 256 calories, 4.3g protein, 11.3g carbohydrates, 12.4g fat, 2.7g fiber, 0mg cholesterol, 64mg sodium, 385mg potassium.

Arugula Salad

Preparation Time: 5 minutes
Cooking Time: 0 minutes
Servings: 4
Ingredients:

- 4 cup arugula leaves
- 1 cup zucchini
- ¼ cup pine nuts
- 1 tbsp rice vinegar
- 2 tbsp olive/grapeseed oil
- ¼ cup parmesan cheese, grated
- Black pepper and salt, as desired
- 1 large avocado, sliced

Directions:

1. Peel and slice the avocado. Rinse and dry the arugula leaves, grate the cheese, and slice the zucchini into halves.
2. Combine the arugula, pine nuts, zucchini, oil, vinegar, salt, pepper, and cheese.
3. Toss the salad to mix and portion it onto plates with the avocado slices to serve.

Nutrition: Calories: 257 kcal; **Protein:** 6.1 g; **Carbohydrates:** 6 g; **Fat:** 5 g

Chickpea Salad

Preparation Time: 15 minutes
Cooking Time: 0 minutes
Servings: 4
Ingredients:
- 15 oz. chickpeas, cooked
- 1 zucchini, diced
- ½ of 1 green medium bell pepper, diced
- 1 tbsp fresh parsley

Directions:
1. Chop zucchini and green pepper. Combine each of the fixings into a salad bowl and toss well.
2. Cover the salad to chill for at least 15 minutes in the fridge. Serve when ready.

Nutrition: Calories: 163 kcal; **Protein:** 4 g; **Carbohydrates:** 6 g; **Fat:** 2 g

Chopped Israeli Mediterranean Pasta Salad

Preparation Time: 15 minutes
Cooking Time: 2 minutes
Servings: 8
Ingredients:
- ½ lb. small bow tie or other small pasta
- ⅓ cup cucumber
- ⅓ cup radish
- ⅓ cup zucchini
- ⅓ cup yellow bell pepper
- ⅓ cup orange bell pepper
- ⅓ cup black olives
- ⅓ cup green olives
- ⅓ cup pepperoncini
- ⅓ cup feta cheese
- ⅓ cup fresh thyme leaves
- 1 tsp oregano, dried

Dressing:
- ¼ cup + more, olive oil

Directions:
1. Slice the green olives into halves. Dice the feta and pepperoncini. Finely dice the remainder of the veggies.
2. Prepare a pot of water with the salt, and simmer the pasta until it's al dente (checking at 2 minutes under the listed time). Rinse and drain in cold water.
3. Combine a small amount of oil with the pasta. Add the salt, pepper, oregano, thyme, and veggies. Pour in the rest of the oil, mix and fold in the grated feta.
4. Pop it into the fridge within 2 hours, best if overnight. Taste test and adjust the seasonings to your liking; add fresh thyme.

Nutrition: Calories: 65 kcal; **Protein:** 0.8 g; **Carbohydrates:** 6 g; **Fat:** 8 g

Feta Zucchini Salad

Preparation Time: 5 minutes
Cooking Time: 0 minutes
Servings: 4
Ingredients:
- 2 tbsp balsamic vinegar
- 1.5 tsp basil, freshly minced, or .5 tsp, dried
- .5 tsp salt
- 2 tbsp olive oil
- 1 lb. zucchini
- ¼ cup low-fat feta cheese, crumbled

Directions:
1. Whisk the salt, basil, and vinegar.
2. Slice the zucchini into halves and stir in the feta cheese, and oil to serve.

Nutrition: Calories: 121 kcal; **Protein:** 3 g; **Carbohydrates:** 10 g; **Fat:** 6 g

Tofu Salad

Preparation Time: 10 minutes
Cooking Time: 15 minutes
Servings: 2
Ingredients:
- ½ pack firm tofu
- 2 spelt tortillas
- 1 avocado
- 4 handfuls baby spinach
- 1 handful almonds
- 2 zucchini
- 1 pink grapefruit

Directions:
1. Heat the tortillas in an oven and once warm, bake for 8–10 minutes in the oven.
2. Chop up the zucchini, and tofu and combine this. Put it in the fridge and let it cool.
3. Now chop up the almonds, avocado, and grapefruit. Mix everything well and place nicely around the bowl you had put in the fridge.
4. Enjoy!

Nutrition: Calories: 110 kcal; **Protein:** 36 g; **Carbohydrates:** 19 g; **Fat:** 11 g

Minty Olives and Zucchini Salad

Preparation Time: 10 minutes
Cooking Time: 0 minutes
Servings: 4
Ingredients:
- 1 cup Kalamata olives
- 1 cup black olives
- 1 cup zucchini

- 4 zucchini
- 2 tbsp oregano, chopped
- 1 tbsp mint, chopped
- 2 tbsp balsamic vinegar
- ¼ cup olive oil
- 2 tsp Italian herbs, dried

Directions:
1. In a salad bowl, mix the olives with the zucchini and the rest of the ingredients, toss, and serve cold.

Nutrition: Calories: 190 kcal; **Protein:** 4.6 g; **Carbohydrates:** 9 g; **Fat:** 8.1 g

Persimmon Salad

Preparation Time: 10 minutes
Cooking Time: 0 minutes
Servings: 4
Ingredients:
- Seeds from 1 pomegranate
- 2 persimmons, cored and sliced
- 5 cups baby arugula
- 4 navel oranges, cut into segments
- ¼ cup white vinegar
- ⅓ cup olive oil
- 3 tbsp pine nuts
- 1 and ½ tsp orange zest, grated
- 2 tbsp orange juice
- 1 tbsp coconut sugar
- ½ shallot, chopped
- A pinch of cinnamon powder

Directions:
1. In a salad bowl, combine the pomegranate seeds with persimmons, arugula, and oranges, and toss. In another bowl, combine the vinegar with the oil, pine nuts, orange zest, orange juice, coconut sugar, shallot, and cinnamon, whisk well, add to the salad, toss and serve as a side dish.

Nutrition: Calories: 310 kcal; **Protein:** 7 g; **Carbohydrates:** 33 g; **Fat:** 16 g

Olives and Lentils Salad

Preparation Time: 10 minutes
Cooking Time: 0 minutes
Servings: 2
Ingredients:
- ⅓ cup green lentils canned
- 1 tbsp olive oil
- 2 cups baby spinach
- 1 cup black olives
- 2 tbsp sunflower seeds
- 1 tbsp Dijon mustard
- 2 tbsp balsamic vinegar
- 2 tbsp olive oil

Directions:
1. Mix the lentils with the spinach, olives, and the rest of the ingredients in a salad bowl, toss and serve cold.

Nutrition: Calories: 279 kcal; **Protein:** 12 g; **Carbohydrates:** 6.9 g; **Fat:** 5.5 g

Avocado Side Salad

Preparation Time: 10 minutes
Cooking Time: 0 minutes
Servings: 4
Ingredients:
- 4 blood oranges, slice into segments
- 2 tbsp olive oil
- A pinch of red pepper, crushed
- 2 avocados, peeled, cut into wedges
- 1 and ½ cups baby arugula

Directions:
1. Mix the oranges with the oil, red pepper, avocados, arugula, and almonds in a bowl, and then serve.

Nutrition: Calories: 146 kcal; **Protein:** 15 g; **Carbohydrates:** 8 g; **Fat:** 7 g

Broccoli Salad

Preparation Time: 15 minutes
Cooking Time: 20 minutes
Servings: 4
Ingredients:
For the Salad:
- Kosher salt
- 3 broccoli heads
- ¼ cup almond, toasted
- 2 tbsp fresh chives

For the dressing:
- 1 tbsp mayonnaise
- 3 tbsp apple cider
- 1 tbsp Dijon mustard
- Kosher salt
- Black paper, ground

Directions:

1. Heat 6 cups of salted water in a medium pot. Then prepare a large bowl with ice water. Mix in the broccoli florets and cook until tender. Take it out from the pan, then transfer it to the bowl with ice water. When it cools down, drain the broccoli.
2. Whisk all the dressing ingredients and season it well to your desired taste. Then mix all the salad ingredients in a separate bowl and pour the dressing. Toss it well until fully coated. Let it chill before serving.

Nutrition: Calories: 150 kcal; **Protein:** 19 g; **Carbohydrates:** 5 g; **Fat:** 2 g

Tabbouleh Salad

Preparation Time: 20 minutes
Cooking Time: 15 minutes
Servings: 4
Ingredients:

- 2 cups water, filtered
- 1 cup millet, rinsed
- ⅓ cup extra-virgin olive oil
- 1½ tsp Himalayan pink salt, divided
- 2 large zucchini, rinsed and finely diced
- 3 scallions, white parts only, rinsed and thinly sliced
- ½ English cucumber, rinsed and finely diced
- ¾ cup fresh mint, rinsed and finely chopped
- 1½ cup fresh parsley, rinsed and finely chopped

Directions:

1. Boil water over high heat. Add the millet and turn the heat to low. Cover the pan and cook for 15 minutes.
2. Remove the pan from the heat and mash the millet with a fork. Let cool with the lid off for 15 minutes. It should be firm but not crunchy or mushy.
3. Meanwhile, in a small bowl, whisk the olive oil, and ½ tsp of salt. Let sit.
4. In a large bowl, combine the zucchini, scallions, cucumber, mint, and parsley. Add the cooled millet. Pour the dressing over and mix well. Taste and season with the remaining 1 tsp of salt, as needed.

Nutrition: Calories: 360 kcal; **Protein:** 8 g; **Carbohydrates:** 44 g; **Fat:** 20 g

Guacamole Salad

Preparation Time: 10 minutes
Cooking Time: 0 minute
Servings: 2

Ingredients:

- 2 avocados, halved and pitted
- ½ cup fresh cilantro, rinsed and chopped
- Juice of ½ lime
- 1 slice jalapeño
- ½ tsp Himalayan pink salt
- 1 zucchini, rinsed and diced

Directions:

1. Take the avocado flesh into a medium bowl. Stir in the cilantro, lime juice, cayenne, and salt. Mash everything until smooth.
2. Add the zucchini, mix well, and serve.

Nutrition: Calories: 450 kcal; **Protein:** 5 g; **Carbohydrates:** 27 g; **Fat:** 30 g

Buckwheat Salad

Preparation Time: 10 minutes
Cooking Time: 15 minutes
Servings: 2
Ingredients:

- 1 cup raw buckwheat, rinsed
- 2 cup water
- 2 handfuls fresh baby spinach leaves, rinsed
- Handful fresh basil leaves, rinsed
- 2 scallions, white parts only, rinsed and chopped
- Himalayan pink salt
- Black pepper, freshly ground
- ¼ cup extra-virgin olive oil
- 2 tbsp mixed sprouts, rinsed
- 1 ripe avocado, peeled, pitted, and sliced
- 1½ oz. low-fat feta cheese (optional)

Directions:

1. Mix the buckwheat and water, then bring it to a boil over high heat. Reduce the heat to simmer and cook for 15 minutes, or until soft. Remove from the heat and let cool.
2. Meanwhile, in a food processor, combine the baby spinach, basil, scallions, and process for 30 seconds. Stir the herb mixture into the cooled buckwheat.
3. Arrange the buckwheat on a platter. Drizzle with the olive oil. Top with the sliced avocado, crumble the feta over top (if using), and serve.

Nutrition: Calories: 385 kcal; **Protein:** 6 g; **Carbohydrates:** 43 g; **Fat:** 24 g

Mixed Sprouts Salad

Preparation Time: 10 minutes
Cooking Time: 0 minute
Servings: 2
Ingredients:

- 1–2 tbsp coconut oil
- Handful fresh chives, rinsed and chopped
- Handful fresh dill, rinsed and chopped
- Handful fresh parsley, rinsed and chopped
- ½ tsp Himalayan pink salt
- ½ tsp black pepper, freshly ground
- 1 scallion, rinsed and chopped
- 1 cucumber, rinsed and chopped
- ½ cup mixed sprouts of choice (alfalfa, radish, broccoli, mung bean, cress, etc.), rinsed

Directions:
1. In a blender, combine the coconut oil, chives, dill, parsley, salt, and pepper, and blend until mainly smooth.
2. Transfer to a medium bowl. Stir in the scallion, cucumber, and sprouts to coat, and serve.

Nutrition: Calories: 168 kcal; **Protein:** 5 g; **Carbohydrates:** 12 g; **Fat:** 14 g

Sweet Potato Salad

Preparation Time: 15 minutes
Cooking Time: 5 minutes
Servings: 2
Ingredients:
For the dressing:
- ½ cup sesame oil
- 2 tbsp coconut oil
- 2 tbsp light soy sauce
- 1 tbsp coconut sugar or raw honey

For the salad:
- 5 ½ oz. fresh baby spinach leaves, rinsed
- 1 zucchini, chopped
- 1 tbsp coconut oil
- 1 large sweet potato, scrubbed, peeled, and diced

Directions:
To make the dressing:
1. In a small bowl, whisk the sesame oil, coconut oil, soy sauce, and coconut sugar until blended. Set aside.

To make the salad:
1. In a large salad bowl, gently toss together the baby spinach, and zucchini. Set aside.
2. In a small skillet over medium heat, heat the coconut oil. Add the sweet potato and cook for 3–5 minutes, stirring, until golden brown. Using a slotted spoon, add the sweet potato to the salad and gently stir to combine. Pour the dressing over the salad, gently toss again to coat, and serve.

Nutrition: Calories: 150 kcal; **Protein:** 8 g; **Carbohydrates:** 20 g; **Fat:** 12 g

Waldorf Salad

Preparation Time: 15 minutes plus overnight to soak
Cooking Time: 0 minute
Servings: 2
Ingredients:
For the dressing:
- 1 ripe avocado, peeled and pitted
- 1 tsp Dijon mustard
- ½ tsp Himalayan pink salt
- Black pepper, freshly ground

For the salad:
- 2 cup chickpeas, canned, rinsed and drained, or cooked, drained, and cooled
- 1 cup sunflower seeds, soaked in filtered water overnight, drained
- 2 apples, rinsed, cored, and chopped
- 1 celery stalk, rinsed and diced
- 1–2 tsp fresh dill, chopped and rinsed

Directions:
To make the dressing:
1. In a small bowl, using a fork, mash together the avocado, mustard, salt, pepper. Set aside

To make the salad:
1. In a large bowl, stir together the chickpeas, sunflower seeds, and dressing until well combined. Stir in the apples and celery. Top with the fresh dill and serve.

Nutrition: Calories: 700 kcal; **Protein:** 6 g; **Carbohydrates:** 22 g; **Fat:** 10 g

Radish and Olives Salad

Preparation Time: 5 minutes
Cooking Time: 0 minutes
Servings: 4
Ingredients:
- 1 lb. radishes, cubed
- 2 tbsp balsamic vinegar
- 2 tbsp olive oil
- 1 cup black olives, pitted and halved
- A pinch black pepper

Directions:
1. Mix radishes with the other ingredients in a large salad bowl, toss, and serve as a side dish.

Nutrition: Calories: 123 kcal; **Protein:** 1.3 g; **Carbohydrates:** 6.9 g; **Fat:** 10.8 g

Vegetable and Sides

Basil Olives Mix

Preparation Time: 5 minutes
Cooking Time: 0 minutes
Servings: 4
Ingredients:

- 2 tbsp olive oil
- 1 tbsp balsamic vinegar
- A pinch black pepper
- 4 cups corn
- 2 cups black olives, pitted and halved
- ½ cup zucchini, halved
- 1 tbsp basil, chopped
- 1 tbsp jalapeno, chopped
- 2 cups romaine lettuce, shredded

Directions:

1. Mix the corn with the olives, lettuce, and the other ingredients in a large bowl, toss well, divide between plates and have it as a side dish.

Nutrition: Calories: 290 kcal; **Protein:** 6.2 g; **Carbohydrates:** 37.6 g; **Fat:** 16.1 g

White Bean Dip

Preparation Time: 5 minutes
Cooking Time: 0 minutes
Portions: 4
INGREDIENTS

1. 1 1/2 cups of cooked cannellini beans, drained and rinsed
2. 2 tbsp extra-virgin olive oil
3. 1/2 teaspoon sea salt
4. freshly ground black pepper
5. 2 to 4 tablespoons water, if needed
6. 2 tablespoons torn fresh basil leaves
7. 2 teaspoons fresh rosemary leaves

DIRECTION:

1. In a food processor, pulse the cannellini beans, olive oil, and zest, salt, and pepper until combined. With the food processor running, slowly add the water and process until smooth. Blend in the fresh herbs, if desired.
2. Serve with veggies or pita.

NUTRITION: Calories: 1606 Total Fat: 8g Total Carbohydrates: 14g Protein: 6g

Artichoke and Kale Stuffed Mushrooms

Preparation Time: 15 minutes
Cooking Time: 28 minutes
Servings: 4
Ingredients:

- 16 large white button mushrooms, stemmed
- 2 tsp olive oil
- 1 cup water-packed artichoke hearts, canned and chopped
- 2 cups kale, finely shredded
- 1 tsp fresh basil, chopped
- 1 tsp fresh oregano, chopped
- ⅛ tsp sea salt

Directions:

1. Preheat the oven to 375°F (190°C).
2. On a baking sheet, hollow-side up to arrange the mushroom caps.
3. Heat the olive oil in a large skillet over medium-high heat.
4. Add the artichoke hearts, kale, basil, oregano, and sea salt. Sauté until the kale is wilted, about 5 minutes.
5. Squeeze the liquid out of the filling into the skillet with the back of a spoon and divide the mixture evenly among the mushroom caps.
6. Bake until the mushrooms are tender, about 20 minutes. Serve warm.

Nutrition: Calories: 75 kcal; **Protein:** 5 g; **Fat:** 3 g; **Carbohydrates:** 11 g

Spinach and Cheese Frittata

Preparation Time: 15 minutes
Cooking Time: 30 minutes
Portions: 4

INGREDIENTS:
1. 2 tablespoons extra virgin olive oil
2. 6 large eggs
3. 2 tablespoons milk
4. 1/3 cup grated Parmesan cheese
5. 1/4 teaspoon salt
6. 1/8 teaspoon freshly ground pepper
7. Zucchini, about 2 tablespoons chopped, optional
8. 8 ounces fresh spinach
9. 2 ounces goat cheese

DIRECTION:
1. Whisk together eggs, milk, salt, pepper
2. In a medium mixing bowl, whisk together the eggs, milk, and Parmesan cheese. mix in the salt and pepper. Set aside.
3. Heat olive oil in an oven-proof, stick-free skillet on medium heat. Sauté until translucent, about 4-5 minutes. Add the zucchini (if using) and cook a minute more.
4. Add the spinach a handful at a time. As the fresh spinach begins to wilt and there is more room in the pan, add more of the fresh chopped spinach to the pan.
5. Once the spinach has wilted, spread the mixture out evenly on bottom of the pan. Pour the egg Parmesan mixture over the spinach.
6. Use a spatula to lift up the spinach mixture along the sides of the pan to let egg mixture flow underneath.
7. Sprinkle bits of goat cheese over the top of the frittata mixture.
8. Lower the heat to low and cover the pan. Let cook on the stovetop 10 to 13 minutes, until all but the center of the frittata is set. (You may need to check a few times, to see how well the frittata is setting.) The center should still be wiggly. Pre-heat the broiler

9. Set the oven rack in the top third of the oven. Broil for like 3 to 4 minutes until the top is golden.
10. Remove it from the oven with oven mitts and allow it to cool for several minutes.

NUTRITION: Calories: 131 Total Fat: 6g Total Carbohydrates: 10g Protein: 4g

Baked Broccoli Frittata

Preparation Time: 5 minutes
Cooking Time: 45 minutes
Portions: 4

INGREDIENTS:
1. tablespoon olive oil
2. ¼ cup chopped parsley
3. 2 cups finely chopped broccoli
4. ½ teaspoon dry basil
5. ¼ cup grated parmesan cheese
6. ¼ teaspoon salt
7. 1 teaspoon pepper
8. 6 eggs
9. 2 egg whites

DIRECTION:
1. Heat oil in a wide non-stick frying pan over medium heat.
2. Stir in parsley, broccoli, and basil. Continue cooking, stirring often, until broccoli is bright green (about 3 minutes).
3. Remove from heat and stir in salt, pepper, and 2 tablespoons of the cheese.
4. In a large bowl, beat eggs and egg whites until well blended. Stir in broccoli mixture.
5. Spray a shallow 2-quart baking dish with cooking spray. Pour the broccoli mixture into the dish. Sprinkle evenly with the remaining Parmesan cheese.
6. Bake, uncovered, in a 350-degree oven until frittata is firm in center when touched (25 to 30 minutes).

NUTRITION: Calories: 304 Total Fat: 10g Total Carbohydrates: 31g Protein: 19g

Farro Panzanella

Preparation Time: 20 minutes
Cooking Time: 45 minutes
Portions: 4

INGREDIENTS:

1. 3/4 cup farro
2. 1 medium butternut squash -peeled and diced into 1-inch cubes
3. 1/2 lb. shiitake Mushrooms -sliced
4. 1 tbsp fresh thyme leaves
5. 1/3 cup white wine -dry
6. 3/4 cup cannellini beans -cooked
7. 3/4 cup heirloom zucchini -halved
8. 1/2 baguette or whole wheat bread
9. 1/4 cup toasted pine nuts -for garnish
10. 1/3 cup of dried cranberries -for garnish (voluntary)
11. 1 bunch Genoese Basil (leaves only)
12. 2 tbsp extra virgin olive oil
13. 1 pinch sea salt - or to taste
14. 1/3 cup mixed fresh herbs - chives, basil, oregano and sage

DIRECTION:

1. To minutes, combine the basil leaves, pine nuts and olive oil. Puree in the bowl of a food processor until smooth. Season to taste, and if the sauce needs to be stretched, add a splash of water. Keep it refrigerated until you're ready to use it.
2. Preheat the oven to 400 degrees Fahrenheit.
3. Toss the butternut squash cubes with a drizzle of olive oil, a big teaspoon of sea and salt in a large mixing dish. Spread them out in a big baking dish lined with parchment paper so they don't touch. Roast for 45 minutes, or until softened and the edges begin to caramelize.
4. A medium saucepan of water should be brought to a rolling boil. Season with a pinch of salt before adding the farro. Simmer for about 20 minutes, or until the pasta is al dente, or slightly chewy. Rinse carefully with water after straining in a colander. Remove from the equation.

5. In the meantime, preheat a big skillet over medium heat. Combine a pinch of salt, and a drizzle of olive oil (or about 1 tablespoon of water) in a mixing bowl. Toss well to coat and cook for a few minutes, or until transparent. Toss in the chopped mushrooms and a splash of white wine. Allow it boil until the mushrooms have wilted and the liquid has nearly completely reduced, then add the fresh thyme. Season with a pinch of sea salt.
6. 3/4 of the pesto sauce, cooked farro, cannellini beans, cooked shiitake mushrooms, and roughly 3/4 of the roasted squash go into a large mixing bowl (reserve some for garnish If you like). Slice or tear the bread into bite-size pieces, then carefully fold everything together with a spatula until everything is well combined.
7. Season with salt and pepper to taste, then transfer to a serving plate. Serve with the reserved squash and the leftover pesto drizzled on top.
8. Serve warm, garnished with toasted pine nuts, herbs, and cranberries..

NUTRITION: Calories: 260 Total Fat: 10g Total Carbohydrates: 33g Protein: 8g

Ratatouille

Preparation Time: 10 minutes
Cooking Time: 30 minutes
Portions: 4

INGREDIENTS:

1. 1 Tbsp, olive oil
2. 1 medium eggplant
3. 2 large zucchinis
4. 1 red bell pepper
5. 2 cups diced zucchini
6. 1 Tbsp, chopped fresh basil leaves

DIRECTION:

1. Place a medium size stockpot over medium low heat. Add oil and all the ingredients chopped. Cook for 10 to 20 minutes

2. Cover and refrigerate overnight or serve immediately, garnished parmesan cheese and basil

NUTRITION: Calories: 127 Total Fat: 4g Total Carbohydrates: 17g Protein: 4g

Zucchini Bulgur

Preparation Time: 7 minutes
Cooking Time: 20 minutes
Servings: 2
Ingredients:
- ½ cup bulgur
- 1 tsp zucchini paste
- 2 tbsp coconut oil
- 1 ½ cup chicken stock

Directions:
1. Toss coconut oil in the pan and melt it.
2. Then add bulgur and stir well.
3. Cook bulgur in coconut oil for 3 minutes.
4. Then add zucchini paste and mix up bulgur until homogenous.
5. Add chicken stock.
6. Close the lid and cook bulgur for 15 minutes over the medium heat.
7. The cooked bulgur should soak all liquid.

Nutrition: Calories: 257 kcal; **Protein:** 5.2 g; **Carbohydrates:** 30.2 g; **Fat:** 14.5 g

Minestrone

Preparation Time: 20 minutes
Cooking Time: 45 minutes
Portions: 4
INGREDIENTS:
1. 2 tablespoons extra-virgin olive oil
2. 2 stalks celery, diced
3. 1 large carrot, diced
4. 1/3-pound green beans, trimmed and cut into 1/2-inch pieces (about 1 1/2 cups)
5. 6 cups low-sodium chicken broth
6. 1 15-ounce can low-sodium kidney beans, drained and rinsed
7. 1 cup elbow pasta
8. 1/3 cup of finely grated parmesan cheese
9. 2 tbsp chopped fresh basil

10. 1 teaspoon dried oregano
11. 1 teaspoon dried basil
12. Kosher salt and freshly ground pepper
13. 1 28-ounce can no-salt-add diced zucchini
14. 1 14-ounce can crush zucchini

DIRECTION:
1. In a large pot, heat the olive oil over medium-high heat. Cook, stirring occasionally, about 4 minutes. Cook for 30 seconds. Cook, stirring occasionally, until the celery and carrots begin to soften, about 5 minutes.
2. Cook for 3 minutes more after adding the green beans, dried oregano and basil, 3/4 teaspoon salt, and pepper to taste.
3. Bring the chopped and crushed zucchini, as well as the chicken broth, to a boil in the pot. Reduce the heat to medium low and continue to cook for another 10 minutes.
4. Cook, stirring occasionally, until the kidney beans and pasta are soft, about 10 minutes.
5. Season with salt and pepper. Pour into bowls and top with parmesan and basil leaves.

NUTRITION: Calories: 203 Total Fat: 1g Total Carbohydrates: 40g Protein: 9g

Mushroom Barley Soup

Preparation Time: 15 minutes
Cooking Time: 30 minutes
Portions: 4
INGREDIENTS:
1. ½ cup chopped celery
2. 1 pound sliced fresh mushrooms
3. 6 cups chicken broth
4. ¾ cup barley
5. salt and pepper to taste
6. ¼ cup olive oil
7. ¾ cup diced carrots

DIRECTION:
1. In a large soup pot, heat the oil over medium heat. Cook and whisk in the carrots, and celery. Cook for a few minutes after adding the mushrooms.

2. Add the chicken stock and barley to the pot. Bring to a boil, then reduce to a low heat setting. Cover and cook for 50 minutes, or until barley is cooked. Before serving, season with salt and pepper.

NUTRITION: Calories: 198 Total Fat: 9g Total Carbohydrates: 24g Protein: 5.8g

Roasted Butternut Squash with Apples

Preparation Time: 10 minutes
Cooking Time: 20 minutes
Portions: 4
INGREDIENTS:
- 2 tbsp oliva oil
- 1 tbsp cinnamon
- 1 butternut squash peeled, seeded, cubes
- 3 medium apples peeled, cubes

DIRECTION:
1. Preheat oven to 400 degrees Fahrenheit. Coat a large, rimmed baking sheet with cooking spray before lining it with foil. In a single layer, arrange the squash and apples. Over the top, drizzle the oil and toss to coat. Cinnamon should be sprinkled on top.
2. Bake for 25 minutes in a preheated oven, stirring once or twice during that time. If preferred, top with more cinnamon and serve right away!

NUTRITION: Calories: 175 Total Fat: 8g Total Carbohydrates: 28g Protein: 2g

Buckwheat Cereal with Mushrooms

Preparation Time: 15 minutes
Cooking Time: 40 minutes
Portions: 4
INGREDIENTS:
2. 1 cup buckwheat groats
3. 1 tablespoon olive oil, or to taste
4. 1 carrot, diced
5. ½ pound mushrooms, diced
6. 1 tablespoon butter
7. 2 cups water
8. A pinch of sea salt
9. A pinch of black pepper

DIRECTION:
2. Rinse buckwheat and drain. Heat a nonstick skillet over medium heat and cook in buckwheat for about 5 minutes or until toasted; transfer to a large bowl and set aside.
3. Add olive oil to the skillet and cook in carrots for about 10 minutes or until tender; stir in mushrooms and cook for about 5 minutes.
4. In a pot set over medium heat, melt butter and stir in buckwheat; add in salt, pepper and water and bring a gentle boil. Simmer for about 20 minutes and then serve right away.

NUTRITION: Calories: 185 Total Fat: 7.5g Total Carbohydrates: 7.5g Protein: 6g

Sweet Potato Home Fries

Preparation Time: 15 minutes or fewer
Cooking Time: 7 to 8 hours on low
Portions: 4–6

INGREDIENTS:
1. 3 tbsp. extra-virgin olive oil, plus more for coating the slow cooker
2. 2 pounds sweet potatoes, diced
3. 1 red bell pepper, seeded and diced
4. 1 tsp. sea salt
5. 1 tsp. dried rosemary, minced
6. ½ tsp. freshly ground black pepper

DIRECTION:
- Coat the slow cooker with a thin layer of olive oil.
- Put the sweet potatoes in the slow cooker, along with the red bell pepper. Drizzle the olive oil as evenly as possible over the vegetables.
- Sprinkle in salt, rosemary, and pepper. Toss evenly to coat the sweet potatoes in the oil and seasonings.
- Cover the cooker and set to low. Cook for 7 to 8 hours and serve.

NUTRITION: Calories: 296 Total Fat: 11 g Total Carbohydrates: 48 g Sugar: 10 g Fiber: 7 g Protein: 4 g Sodium: 0.705 g.

Roasted Carrots

Preparation Time: 10 minutes
Cooking Time: 40 minutes
Servings: 4
Ingredients:
- 8 carrots, peeled and cut
- 1 tsp thyme, chopped
- 2 tbsp extra-virgin olive oil
- ½ tsp rosemary, chopped
- ¼ tsp pepper, ground
- ½ tsp salt

Directions:
1. Preheat your oven to 425°F.
2. Mix the carrots by tossing them in a bowl with rosemary, thyme, pepper, and salt. Spread on your baking sheet.
3. Roast for 40 minutes. The carrots should be browning and tender.

Nutrition: Calories: 126 kcal; **Protein:** 2 g; **Carbohydrates:** 16 g; **Fat:** 6 g

Moroccan Style Couscous

Preparation Time: 10 minutes
Cooking Time: 10 minutes
Servings: 4
Ingredients:
- 1 cup yellow couscous
- ½ tsp cardamom, ground
- 1 cup chicken stock
- 1 tbsp butter
- 1 tsp salt
- ½ tsp red pepper

Directions:
1. Toss butter in the pan and melt it.
2. Add couscous and roast it for 1 minute over the high heat.
3. Then add ground cardamom, salt, and red pepper. Stir it well.
4. Pour the chicken stock and bring the mixture to boil.

5. Simmer couscous for 5 minutes with the closed lid.

Nutrition: Calories: 196 kcal; **Protein:** 5.9 g; **Carbohydrates:** 35 g; **Fat:** 3.4 g

Roasted Curried Cauliflower

Preparation Time: 5 minutes
Cooking Time: 30 minutes
Servings: 4
Ingredients:
- 1 large head cauliflower, cut into florets
- 1 and ½ tbsp olive oil
- 1 tsp cumin seeds
- 1 tsp mustard seeds
- ¾ tsp salt

Directions:
1. Preheat your oven to 375°F.
2. Grease a baking sheet with cooking spray.
3. Take a bowl and place all ingredients.
4. Toss to coat well.
5. Arrange the vegetable on a baking sheet.
6. Roast for 30 minutes.
7. Serve and enjoy!

Nutrition: Calories: 67 kcal; **Protein:** 2 g; **Carbohydrates:** 4 g; **Fat:** 6 g

Caramelized Pears

Preparation Time: 5 minutes
Cooking Time: 35 minutes
Servings: 4
Ingredients:
- 2 firm red pears, cored and quartered
- 1 tbsp olive oil
- Salt and pepper, to taste

Directions:
1. Preheat your oven to 425°F.
2. Place the pears on a baking tray.
3. Drizzle with olive oil.
4. Season with salt and pepper.
5. Bake in the oven for 35 minutes.
6. Serve and enjoy!

Nutrition: Calories: 101 kcal; **Protein:** 1 g; **Carbohydrates:** 17 g; **Fat:** 4 g

Ethiopian Cabbage Delight

Preparation Time: 15 minutes
Cooking Time: 6–8 hours
Servings: 6
Ingredients:
- ½ cup water
- 1 head green cabbage, cored and chopped
- 1 lb. sweet potatoes, peeled and chopped
- 3 carrots, peeled and chopped
- 1 tsp extra virgin olive oil

- ½ tsp turmeric, ground
- ½ tsp cumin, ground
- ¼ tsp ginger, ground

Directions:
1. Add water to your Slow Cooker.
2. Take a medium bowl and add cabbage, carrots, sweet potatoes, and mix.
3. Add olive oil, turmeric, ginger, cumin and toss until the veggies are fully coated.
4. Transfer veggie mix to your Slow Cooker.
5. Cover and cook on LOW for 6–8 hours.
6. Serve and enjoy!

Nutrition: Calories: 155 kcal; **Protein:** 4 g; **Carbohydrates:** 35 g; **Fat:** 2 g

Cool Garbanzo and Spinach Beans

Preparation Time: 5–10 minutes
Cooking Time: 0 minute
Servings: 4
Ingredients:
- 12 oz. garbanzo beans
- 1 tbsp olive oil
- ½ tsp cumin
- 10 oz. spinach, chopped

Directions:
1. Take a skillet and add olive oil.
2. Place it over medium-low heat.
3. Add garbanzo and cook for 5 minutes.
4. Stir in cumin, garbanzo beans, spinach and season with sunflower seeds.
5. Use a spoon to smash gently.
6. Cook thoroughly.
7. Serve and enjoy!

Nutrition: Calories: 90 kcal; **Protein:** 4 g; **Carbohydrates:** 11 g; **Fat:** 4 g

Avocado Cucumber Sushi

Preparation Time: 20 minutes
Cooking Time: 15 minutes
Servings: 4
Ingredients:
- 1½ cups dry quinoa
- 6 nori sheets
- 3 avocados, halved, pitted, and sliced thin, divided
- 1 small cucumber, halved, seeded, and cut into matchsticks, divided
- 3 cups water, plus additional for rolling
- ½ tsp salt
- Coconut aminos, for dipping (optional)

Directions:
1. In a fine-mesh sieve, rinse the quinoa.

2. Add the rinsed quinoa, water, and salt into a medium pot, bring to a boil over high heat. Reduce the heat to low. Cover and simmer for 15 minutes. Use a fork to fluff the quinoa.
3. Lay out 1 nori sheet on a cutting board, spread ½ cup of quinoa over the sheet, leaving 2 to 3 inches uncovered at the top.
4. Put 5 or 6 avocado slices across the bottom of the nori sheet in a row. Add 5 or 6 cucumber matchsticks on top.
5. From the bottom, roll up the nori sheet tightly. Dab the uncovered top with water to seal the roll.
6. Cut the sushi roll into 6 pieces.
7. Repeat with the remaining 5 nori sheets, quinoa, and vegetables.
8. After all is done, serve the sushi with the coconut aminos (if using).

Nutrition: Calories: 240 kcal; **Protein:** 8 g; **Carbohydrates:** 18 g; **Fat:** 6 g

Exuberant Sweet Potatoes

Preparation Time: 5 minutes
Cooking Time: 7–8 hours
Servings: 4
Ingredients:
- 6 sweet potatoes, washed and dried

Directions:
1. Loosely ball up 7–8 pieces of aluminum foil in the bottom of your Slow Cooker, covering about half of the surface area.
2. Prick each potato 6–8 times using a fork.
3. Wrap each potato with foil and seal them.
4. Place wrapped potatoes in the cooker on top of the foil bed.
5. Place lid and cook on LOW for 7–8 hours.
6. Use tongs to remove the potatoes and unwrap them.
7. Serve and enjoy!

Nutrition: **Calories:** 129 kcal; **Carbohydrates:** 30 g; **Protein:** 2 g; **Fat:** 0 g

Kale, Mushroom, Walnut, and Avocado

Preparation Time: 10 minutes
Cooking Time: 15 minutes
Servings: 2–3
Ingredients:
- 6 kale leaves, chopped
- 10 walnuts, crushed
- ¼ red bell pepper, diced
- ½ zucchini, sliced
- 20 mushrooms, sliced
- ½–1 tbsp avocado oil

Dressing:
- 1 tbsp key lime juice
- 1 tbsp sesame oil
- 1 zucchini
- ⅛ tsp sea salt
- ¼ avocado

Directions:
1. **Dressing:** Blend the lime juice, sesame oil, zucchini, salt, and avocado together until smooth. Sauté the mushrooms in the avocado oil.
2. Let cool afterward. Mix the kale, walnuts, pepper, zucchini, and mushrooms together. Pour the dressing into the salad, then toss it well until it evenly coats the entire salad.

Nutrition: Calories: 87 kcal; **Protein:** 10 g; **Carbohydrates:** 22 g; **Fat:** 1 g

Mix-Mix Alkaline Veggie

Preparation Time: 5 minutes
Cooking Time: 10 minutes
Servings: 2
Ingredients:
- 15 kale leaves, chopped
- 1 cup watercress leaves
- 1 cucumber, diced
- 2 tbsp fresh dill, finely chopped
- 5–10 olives, sliced
- ¼ red bell pepper, chopped
- ¼ green bell pepper, chopped
- 1 tbsp 100% date sugar syrup
- 3 tbsp water
- ⅛ tsp sea salt

Directions:
1. Mix the date sugar syrup, water, and salt together. Stir the remaining ingredients together in a bowl. Massage in date syrup mix with the vegetables.
2. Toss and serve.

Nutrition: Calories: 102 kcal; **Protein:** 3 g; **Carbohydrates:** 6 g; **Fat:** 3 g

Seasoned Wild Rice

Preparation Time: 5 minutes
Cooking Time: 25 minutes
Servings: 1–2
Ingredients:

- 1 cup wild rice (soak wild rice overnight)
- 2–3 cup water (3 cup water if you didn't soak the rice overnight)
- 1 tbsp coconut oil
- 2 tsp oregano
- ½ tsp sea salt
- 2–3 scallions, chopped
- 1 zucchini, chopped

Directions:

1. Soaking the rice in water overnight reduces the cooking time for the rice.
2. Transfer all the ingredients to a saucepan over high heat and let them come to a boil.
3. Cover the saucepan and reduce to a simmer and allow the water to absorb into the rice. If you soaked the rice overnight, cook the rice for 25 minutes.
4. If you did not soak the rice overnight, cook for 50–60 minutes.

Nutrition: Calories: 220 kcal; **Protein:** 5 g; **Carbohydrates:** 26 g; **Fat:** 4 g

Roasted Large Cap Portobello Mushrooms and Yellow Squash

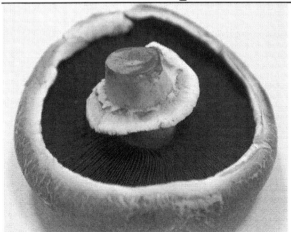

Preparation Time: 10 minutes
Cooking Time: 30 minutes
Servings: 1–2
Ingredients:

- 3 large Portobello mushrooms
- 9 ½ inch slices yellow squash

- Avocado oil (brush on front and back of mushrooms)
- ½ lime
- Spices (coriander, cayenne pepper, oregano, sea salt)

Directions:

1. Pull off the Portobello mushroom stems and scoop out the fins with a spoon. Brush on avocado oil on the front and back of the mushrooms. Squeeze a little lime over the tops of the mushrooms.
2. Sprinkle the spices on the mushrooms and yellow squash but keep the mushrooms and squash separate. Heat oven to 400°F. Place mushrooms on the roasting pan, scooped outside facing up. Cook for 10 minutes.
3. Carefully remove the pan and mushrooms, and add 3 seasoned yellow squash slices to each mushroom top. Put the roasting pan back into the oven. Cook the mushrooms and squash for another 10 minutes. Remove from oven and serve hot.

Nutrition: Calories: 148 kcal; **Protein:** 5.9 g; **Carbohydrates:** 8 g; **Fat:** 8 g

Simply Chayote Squash

Preparation Time: 10 minutes
Cooking Time: 20 minutes
Servings: 1
Ingredients:

- 1 chayote squash
- ¼ tsp coconut oil
- Dash cayenne pepper
- Dash sea salt

Directions:

1. Wash and cut chayote squash in half. The seed can be eaten, and it has a nice texture. Add chayote, oil, and enough water to cover the chayote in a saucepan.
2. Boil for 20 minutes until the fork can penetrate the squash, but the squash should still maintain some firmness. Remove from water. Season it well with cayenne pepper and salt.
3. Serve as a light snack or part of a dish.

Nutrition: Calories: 117 kcal; **Protein:** 4 g; **Carbohydrates:** 12 g; **Fat:** 6 g

Vegetable Medley Sauté

Preparation Time: 10 minutes
Cooking Time: 15 minutes
Servings: 4
Ingredients:

- 1 cup mushrooms, sliced

- 1 zucchini, sliced
- 1 yellow squash, sliced
- 1 red pepper, chopped
- 1 green pepper, chopped
- 2 zucchini, chopped
- ½ cup chayote, finely chopped
- 3 tbsp grape-seed oil or avocado oil
- ⅛ tsp cayenne pepper
- ⅛ tsp sea salt

Directions:
1. Cook the oil in a saucepan over medium heat. Let the oil get hot.
2. Add in mushrooms and sauté for 4 minutes. Add in the rest of the vegetables and spices and sauté for 8–10 minutes.

Nutrition: Calories: 115 kcal; **Protein:** 11 g; **Carbohydrates:** 20 g; **Fat:** 6 g

Desserts

Apple Couscous Pudding

Preparation Time: 10 minutes
Cooking Time: 25 minutes
Servings: 4
Ingredients:

- ½ cup couscous
- ½ cups milk
- ¼ cup apple, cored and chopped
- 2 tbsp stevia
- ½ tsp rose water
- 1 tbsp orange zest, grated

Directions:

1. Heat a pan with the milk over medium heat, add the couscous and the rest of the ingredients, whisk, simmer for 25 minutes, divide into bowls and serve.

Nutrition: Calories: 150 kcal; **Protein:** 4 g; **Carbohydrates:** 7.5 g; **Fat:** 4.5 g

Rice Pudding

Preparation Time: 5 minutes
Cooking Time: 20 minutes
Servings: 4
Ingredients:

- 4 ⅓ cup almond milk, unsweetened
- 3½ oz. brown rice
- 1 tbsp brown sugar, packed
- 2 tbsp pure maple syrup, separated

Directions:

1. Empty milk in a saucepan on the highest heat setting. As it starts to bubble, turn the heat to medium/low, then transfer the rice into the pot.
2. Toss to cover the rice completely. Blend sugar and integrate fully. Toss frequently for 20 minutes or until it reaches the desired thickness.
3. Transfer to serving dishes and drizzle with ½ tbsp each with maple syrup.

Nutrition: Calories: 100 kcal; **Protein:** 6 g; **Carbohydrates:** 22 g; **Fat:** 3 g

Pudding Glass with Banana and Whipped Cream

Preparation Time: 10 minutes
Cooking Time: 8 minutes
Servings: 2
Ingredients:

- 2 portions banana cream pudding mix
- 2 ½ cups rice milk
- 8 oz. soy whipped cream
- 12 oz. vanilla wafers

Directions:

1. Put vanilla wafers in a pan, and in another bowl, mix banana cream pudding and rice milk.
2. Boil the ingredients, blending them slowly.
3. Pour the mixture over the wafers and make 2 or 3 layers.
4. Put the pan in the fridge for one hour and afterward spread the whipped topping over the dessert.
5. Put it back in the fridge for 2 hours and serve it cold in transparent glasses. Serve and enjoy!

Nutrition: Calories: 255 kcal; **Protein:** 3 g; **Carbohydrates:** 13 g; **Fat:** 8 g

Carrot Cake Bites

Preparation Time: 10 minutes
Cooking Time: 0 minutes
Servings: 4
Ingredients:

- 4 baby carrots, peeled and chopped
- ⅛ tsp pure vanilla extract, sugar-free
- ⅓ cup coconut, shredded and unsweetened
- 2 tbsp almond butter, unsalted
- ⅛ tsp cinnamon, ground
- 1 tbsp pure maple syrup
- ⅓ cup gluten-free oats, rolled
- ⅛ tsp salt, iodized

Directions:

1. Thoroughly clean carrots and remove the skins. Chop into big chunks and transfer to a food blender.
9. Pulse for approximately 2 minutes until consistency is slightly chunky. Transfer to a glass dish.
10. Combine coconut and oats in a food blender and pulse for an additional 2 minutes.
11. Empty carrots, almond butter, maple syrup, salt, vanilla extract, and cinnamon in a food blender and pulse for a total of 2 minutes until the batter thickens. Section into 4 pieces and hand roll into spheres.
12. Serve immediately and enjoy!

Nutrition: Calories: 160 kcal; **Protein:** 9 g; **Carbohydrates:** 12 g; **Fat:** 4 g

Pumpkin Peanut Pudding

Preparation Time: 10 minutes
Cooking Time: 0 minutes
Servings: 4
Ingredients:

- ⅛ tsp nutmeg, ground
- ½ cup peanuts, raw and unsalted
- ⅛ tsp salt, iodized
- ⅓ cup pumpkin puree
- ¼ tsp cinnamon, ground
- ⅛ cup pure maple syrup
- ¼ cup almond milk, unsweetened
- ½ tbsp coconut oil, melted
- ⅛ cloves, ground

Directions:

1. Pulse nutmeg, peanuts, salt, pumpkin puree, cinnamon, maple syrup, almond milk, coconut oil, and cloves for approximately 3 minutes.
2. Make sure all ingredients are incorporated. Divide equally into individual glasses or a dish.
3. Serve immediately and enjoy!

Nutrition: Calories: 140 kcal; **Protein:** 2 g; **Carbohydrates:** 18 g; **Fat:** 5 g

Berry Blast

Preparation Time: 15 minutes
Cooking Time: 40 minutes
Servings: 1
Ingredients:

- 4 cups blueberries (2 cups fresh and 2 cups frozen)
- 1 cup rolled oats
- 1 tsp cinnamon
- 2 tbsp all-purpose flour
- 2 tsp olive oil
- 1 tbsp maple syrup

Directions:

1. Coat a pie pan with cooking spray and set it aside. Put the blueberries on the pie plate. Preheat the oven to 250°F.
2. Combine the flour, oil, oats, maple syrup, and cinnamon in a large mixing bowl and whisk until you obtain a grainy mixture.
3. Transfer the oats mixture to the pie pan and bake for 40 minutes until the mixture is golden brown. Serve warm.

Nutrition: Calories: 424 kcal; **Fat:** 10.2 g; **Carbohydrates:** 66.6 g; **Protein:** 4.9 g

Oats and Fruit Bar Cracker

Preparation Time: 15 minutes
Cooking Time: 0 minutes
Servings: 3
Ingredients:

- 1 cup quinoa
- 1 cup oats
- ½ cup figs, dried
- ½ cup honey
- ½ cup almonds, chopped
- ½ cup apricots, dried
- ½ cup wheat germ
- ½ cup pineapple, dried and chopped
- 1 tbsp cornstarch

Directions:

1. Mix the fixing in a mixing bowl until you obtain a well-balanced mixture. Put the batter on a baking tray or plate and flatten it. Ensure that the mixture is at least one inch thick. Let it cool before you cut it into pieces and serve.

Nutrition: Calories: 296 kcal; **Fat:** 3.7 g; **Carbohydrates:** 144.2 g; **Protein:** 5.2 g

Colorful Pops

Preparation Time: 15 minutes
Cooking Time: 0 minutes
Servings: 6
Ingredients:

- 2 cups watermelon, strawberries, and cantaloupe, diced
- 2 cups pure apple juice
- 2 cups fresh blueberries
- 6 craft sticks
- 6 paper cups

Directions:

1. Mix all the fruit in a mixing bowl. Divide the fruit salad into the paper cups and pour the apple juice. Ensure that the apple juice only covers half the paper cup. Deep-freeze the cups for an hour or until they are partially frozen.
2. Remove the cups and add the sticks to the cups, and deep freeze for 1 more hour. Serve them as colorful pops!

Nutrition: Calories: 83 kcal; **Fat:** 0.2 g; **Carbohydrates:** 20.8 g; **Protein:** 0.7 g

Pumpkin Pie

Preparation Time: 15 minutes
Cooking Time: 50 minutes
Servings: 2
Ingredients:

- 1 cup ginger snaps
- 8 oz. pumpkin, canned
- ¼ cup egg whites
- ¼ cup raw brown sugar
- 1 tsp pumpkin pie spice
- 6 oz. skim milk, evaporated
- Cooking spray

Directions:

1. Preheat the oven to 300°F. Oiled a glass pie pan with cooking spray. Crumble the ginger snaps and pat them into the glass pan. Mix the rest of the fixing in a mixing bowl and pour it into the prepared glass pie pan.
2. Bake the dish for fifty minutes or until a knife inserted in the center comes out clean. Transfer the pie pan to the refrigerator and allow it to cool. Serve cold.

Nutrition: Calories: 392 kcal; **Fat:** 16.6 g; **Carbohydrates:** 80.7 g; **Protein:** 20 g

Walnut and Oatmeal Chocolate Chip Cookies

Preparation Time: 15 minutes
Cooking Time: 20 minutes
Servings: 4
Ingredients:

- 1 cup rolled oats
- ¼ cup all-purpose flour
- ¼ cup whole-wheat pastry flour
- ½ tsp cinnamon, ground
- ¼ tsp baking soda
- ¼ tsp salt
- ¼ tsp tahini
- 2 tbsp olive oil
- ½ cup raw brown sugar
- ½ cup maple syrup
- 2 eggs (1 whole and 1 egg white)
- ½ tbsp vanilla extract
- ½ cup bittersweet chocolate chips
- ¼ cup walnuts, chopped

Directions:

1. Place racks in the oven's upper and lower parts and preheat the oven to 300°F. Prepare or arrange two lined baking sheets with parchment paper. Combine the oats, whole-wheat flour, all-purpose flour, baking soda, cinnamon, and salt in a bowl and whisk.
2. Beat oil and tahini in a large mixing bowl and blend until you obtain a paste. Add maple syrup and erythritol to the bowl and continue to beat until you get a well-combined mixture. Note that the mixture will still be slightly grainy.
3. Now, add the vanilla extract, egg white, and whole egg to the bowl and continue to whisk until you obtain a well-combined mixture.
4. Stir in the oat mixture, chocolate chips, and walnuts into the bowl. Wet your hands slightly, roll 1 tbsp of the batter into a small ball, and place it on the baking sheet. Flatten the ball out but ensure that the sides do not crack. Continue with the remaining batter and leave at least a 2-inch space between each cookie.
5. Bake the cookies for 20 minutes or until golden brown. Cool the cookies for 2 minutes before you transfer them onto the wire rack to cool completely.

Nutrition: Calories: 530 kcal; **Fat:** 14.8 g; **Carbohydrates:** 98.6 g; **Protein:** 10.6 g

Apple Dumplings

Preparation Time: 10 minutes
Cooking Time: 30 minutes
Servings: 6
Ingredients:
Dough:

- 1 tbsp olive oil
- 1 tsp honey
- 1 cup whole-wheat flour
- 2 tbsp buckwheat flour
- 2 tbsp rolled oats

Apple filling:

- 6 large tart apples, thinly sliced
- 1 tsp nutmeg
- 2 tbsp honey

Directions:

1. Warm oven to heat at 350°F. Combine flours with oats, honey, and oil in a food processor. Pulse this mixture for few times, then mix until it forms a ball. Wrap it in a plastic sheet.
2. Refrigerate for 2 hours. Mix apples with honey, and nutmeg, then set it aside. Spread the dough into ¼ inch thick sheet. Cut it into 8-inch circles and layer the greased muffin cups with the dough circles.
3. Divide the apple mixture into the muffin cups and seal the dough from the top. Bake

for 30 minutes at 350°F until golden brown. Enjoy.

Nutrition: Calories: 178 kcal; **Fat:** 5.7 g; **Carbs:** 32.4 g; **Protein:** 2.1 g

Banana Delight

Preparation Time: 15 minutes
Cooking Time: 12 minutes
Servings: 4
Ingredients:
- 1 tbsp sodium-free baking powder
- 1 tbsp raw brown sugar
- 1 cup flour
- 1 tbsp oil
- ¼ cup egg substitute
- ½ tsp nutmeg
- 1 cup banana, chopped
- ½ cup soy milk

Directions:
1. In a bowl, mix and stir baking powder, sugar, and flour. Mix oil, egg, and milk, then add nutmeg and banana in a separate bowl. Add the mixture into the bowl of dry ingredients.
2. In a hot frying pan, drop just by tablespoonfuls and fry for about 2 to 3 minutes. Wait until it is golden brown, then drain and serve.

Nutrition: Calories: 210.1 kcal; **Protein:** 5.7 g; **Carbs:** 37.6 g; **Fat:** 7.1 g

Healthy Banana-Choco Ice Cream

Preparation Time: 10 minutes
Cooking Time: 0 minutes
Servings: 4
Ingredients:
- 3 medium bananas, peeled and frozen
- 3 tbsp cocoa powder, unsweetened

Directions:
1. Place all the fixing in a blender and puree until it resembles soft-serve ice cream. Evenly divide into 4 bowls. Serve and enjoy

Nutrition: Calories: 88 kcal; **Protein:** 1.7 g; **Carbs:** 22.6 g; **Fat:** 0.8 g

Healthy Chocolate Mousse

Preparation Time: 10 minutes
Cooking Time: 0 minutes
Servings: 4
Ingredients:

- 1 large, ripe avocado
- ¼ cup almond milk, sweetened
- 1 tbsp coconut oil
- ¼ cup cocoa or cacao powder
- 1 tsp vanilla extract

Directions:
1. Process all the fixing using a food processor until smooth and creamy. Chill within 4 hours. Serve and enjoy.

Nutrition: Calories: 125 kcal; **Protein:** 1.2 g; **Carbs:** 6.9 g; **Fat:** 11.0 g

Almond Rice Pudding

Preparation Time: 25 minutes
Cooking Time: 20 minutes
Servings: 6
Ingredients:
- 3 cups almond milk
- 1 cup white rice
- ¼ cup raw brown sugar
- 1 tsp vanilla
- ¼ tsp almond extract
- Cinnamon
- ¼ cup almonds, toasted

Directions:
1. Mix milk plus rice in a medium saucepan. Bring them to a boil. Reduce heat and simmer for 20 minutes with the lid on until the rice is soft.
2. Remove, then put the sugar, vanilla, almond extract, and cinnamon. Put toasted almonds on top, then serve warm.

Nutrition: Calories: 180 kcal; **Fat:** 1.5 g; **Carbohydrates:** 36 g; Protein: 7 g

Apples and Cream Shake

Preparation Time: 10 minutes
Cooking Time: 0 minutes
Servings: 4
Ingredients:
- 2 cups vanilla low-fat ice cream
- 1 cup apple sauce
- ¼ tsp ground cinnamon
- 1 cup fat-free skim milk

Directions:
1. In a blender container, combine the low-fat ice cream, applesauce, and cinnamon. Cover and blend until smooth. Add fat-free skim milk. Cover and blend until mixed. Pour into glasses. Serve immediately.

Nutrition: Calories: 160 kcal; **Fat:** 3 g; **Carbohydrates:** 27 g; Protein: 6 g

Juices and Smoothies

Mango smoothie

Preparation time: 10 minutes
Servings: 2
Ingredients:
- 1 cup almond milk
- 1 cup mango, cubes
- ½ cup ice cubes

Topping:
- Blueberries
- Mint leaves
- Mango cubes
- Coconut flakes

Directions:
1. Add all the ingredients to a blender and blend until all ingredients are well blended.
2. Pour the smoothie into serving glasses.
3. Serve and enjoy!

Nutrition: Calories: 94 kcal; **Protein:** 1 g; **Carbohydrate:** 21 g; **Fat:** 1 g; **Sugar:** 12 g

Vanilla Turmeric Orange Juice

Preparation Time: 5 minutes
Cooking Time: 0 minutes
Servings: 2
Ingredients:
- 6 oranges, peeled, separated into segments, deseeded
- 2 tsp vanilla extract
- ½ tsp turmeric powder
- 2 cups almond milk, unsweetened
- 1 tsp cinnamon, ground

Directions:
1. Juice the oranges. Add the rest of the ingredients.
2. Pour into glasses and serve.

Nutrition: Calories: 110 kcal; **Protein:** 2.4 g; **Carbohydrates:** 25 g; **Fat:** 1.7 g

Cucumber Kiwi Green Smoothie

Preparation Time: 5 minutes
Cooking Time: 0 minutes
Servings: 2
Ingredients:
- 2 ripe kiwi fruit
- 1 cup cucumber, chopped and seedless
- 1 cup coconut water
- 6 to 8 ice cubes
- ice cubes
- ¼ cup coconut milk, canned
- 2 tbsp cilantro, fresh chopped

Directions:
1. Combine the smoothie ingredients in your high-speed blender.
2. Pulse a few times to cut them up.
3. Blend the mixture on the highest speed setting for 30 to 60 seconds.
4. Pour your finished smoothie into glasses and drink.

Nutrition: Calories: 140 kcal; **Protein:** 1 g; **Carbohydrates:** 24 g; **Fat:** 1.5 g

Tropical Pineapple Kiwi Smoothie

Preparation Time: 5 minutes
Cooking Time: 0 minutes
Servings: 2
Ingredients:
- 1 ½ cup pineapple, frozen
- 1 ripe kiwi, peeled and chopped
- 1 cup coconut milk
- 6 to 8 ice cubes
- 1 tsp spirulina powder
- 3 tsp lime juice

Directions:
1. Combine the smoothie ingredients in your high-speed blender.
2. Pulse a few times to cut them up.
3. Blend the mixture on the highest speed setting.
4. Pour your finished smoothie into glasses and drink.

Nutrition: Calories: 250 kcal; **Protein:** 8.3 g; **Carbohydrates:** 38.3 g; **Fat:** 27.9 g

Dreamy Yummy Orange Cream Smoothie

Preparation Time: 5 minutes
Cooking Time: 0 minutes
Servings: 2
Ingredients:

- 1 navel orange, peel removed
- 1 cup almond milk
- 6 to 8 ice cubes
- ½ cup coconut milk
- ¼ cup fresh orange juice

Directions:

1. Combine the smoothie ingredients in your high-speed blender.
2. Pulse a few times to cut them up.
3. Blend the mixture on the highest speed setting for 30 to 60 seconds.
4. Pour your finished smoothie into glasses and drink.

Nutrition: Calories: 299 kcal; **Protein:** 3.6 g; **Carbohydrates:** 32.7 g; **Fat:** 28.3 g

Peachy Keen Smoothie

Preparation Time: 5 minutes
Cooking Time: 0 minutes
Servings: 2
Ingredients:

- 1 ½ cups peaches, frozen
- 1 small banana, frozen
- 1 cup almond milk
- 6 to 8 ice cubes
- 2 tbsp raw hemp seeds
- Pinch ginger, ground

Directions:

1. Combine the smoothie ingredients in your high-speed blender.
2. Pulse a few times to cut them up.
3. Blend the mixture on the highest speed setting for 30 to 60 seconds.
4. Pour your finished smoothie into glasses and drink.

Nutrition: Calories: 233 kcal; **Protein:** 1.5 g; **Carbohydrates:** 54.0 g; **Fat:** 11.9 g

Cucumber Melon Smoothie

Preparation Time: 5 minutes
Cooking Time: 0 minutes
Servings: 2
Ingredients:

- 1 ½ cups honeydew, chopped
- 1 cup cucumber, diced and seedless
- 1 cup coconut water, chilled
- 6 to 8 ice cubes

- 2 tbsp fresh mint

Directions:

1. Combine the smoothie ingredients in your high-speed blender.
2. Pulse a few times to cut them up.
3. Blend the mixture on the highest speed setting for 30 to 60 seconds.
4. Pour your finished smoothie into glasses and drink.

Nutrition: Calories: 168 kcal; **Protein:** 2.8 g; **Carbohydrates:** 31.2 g; **Fat:** 0.5 g

Tropical Mango Coconut Smoothie

Preparation Time: 5 minutes
Cooking Time: 0 minutes
Servings: 2
Ingredients:

- 1 ½ cups mango, frozen
- 1 medium banana, frozen
- ½ cup fresh orange juice
- ½ cup coconut milk, canned
- 1 ½ tsp honey

Directions:

1. Combine the smoothie ingredients in your high-speed blender.
2. Pulse a few times to cut them up.
3. Blend the mixture on the highest speed setting for 30 to 60 seconds.
4. Pour your finished smoothie into glasses and drink.

Nutrition: Calories: 554 kcal; **Protein:** 6 g; **Carbohydrates:** 87.4 g; **Fat:** 18.0 g

Blueberry and Strawberry Smoothie

Preparation Time: 5 minutes
Cooking Time: 0 minutes
Servings: 2
Ingredients:

- 6–7 strawberries, sliced
- ½ lb. blueberries
- ½ pint almond milk

Directions:

1. Add all ingredients to a blender jar. Blend until smooth. Add to serving glasses.
2. Serve and enjoy.

Nutrition: Calories: 107 kcal; **Protein:** 2 g; **Carbohydrates:** 17 g; **Fat:** 4 g

Blueberry and Apple Smoothie

Preparation Time: 25 minutes

Cooking Time: 15 minutes
Servings: 4
Ingredients:
- 1 Brae burn apple, or another kind of organic apple
- ½ lb. Brazil nuts
- ½ lb. homemade walnut milk
- ½ lb. blueberries
- ½ lb. approved greens (dandelion greens, turnip greens, watercress, etc.)
- ½ tbsp date sugar or agave syrup

Directions:
1. Combine all the ingredients in a high-speed mixer. Add more water if the mixture is too concentrated.

Nutrition: Calories: 241 kcal; **Protein:** 23.8 g; **Carbohydrates:** 30.2 g; **Fat:** 5.8 g

Blueberry Pie Smoothie

Preparation Time: 20 minutes
Cooking Time: 0 minutes
Servings: 2
Ingredients:
- 1 oz. fresh blueberries
- 1 banana
- 1 glass coconut milk
- ½ lb. amaranth, cooked
- 1 tbsp homemade walnut butter
- 1 tbsp date sugar

Directions:
1. Combine all the ingredients in a high-speed mixer. Add more water if the mixture is too concentrated.

Nutrition: Calories: 413 kcal; **Protein:** 5.8 g; **Carbohydrates:** 62 g; **Fat:** 26.9 g

Cucumber and Carley Green Smoothie

Preparation Time: 10 minutes
Cooking Time: 0 minutes
Servings: 4
Ingredients:
- 1 lb. soft jelly coconut water
- 4 tbsp cucumbers, seeded
- 2–3 limes
- 1 bunch basil or sweet basil leaves

Directions:
1. Mix cucumbers, basil, and lime. If you don't have a juicer, treat them in a grinder with sweet coconut jelly. Transfer in a tall glass and stir in coconut water to make it smooth, and add powdered bromide. Mix well and enjoy.

Nutrition: Calories: 86 kcal; **Protein:** 1 g; **Carbohydrates:** 24.2 g; **Fat:** 0.4 g

Kale and Ginger Smoothie

Preparation Time: 5 minutes
Cooking Time: 0 minute
Servings: 2
Ingredients:
- 2 cup spring water
- 1 cup kale leaves, fresh
- ¼ cup key lime juice
- 1 medium fresh apple, cored
- 1-inch piece ginger, fresh
- 1 cup fresh cucumber, sliced
- 1 tbsp sea moss gel

Directions:
1. Take a high-powered blender, switch it on, and then place all the ingredients inside, in order.
2. Close the blender, then pulses at high speed for 1 minute.

Nutrition: Calories: 65.5 kcal; **Protein:** 0.7 g; **Carbohydrates:** 14.7 g; **Fat:** 0.4 g

Arugula and Cucumber Smoothie

Preparation Time: 5 minutes
Cooking Time: 0 minute
Servings: 2
Ingredients:
- 2 cup spring water
- 1 large bunch callaloo, fresh
- ¼ cup lime juice
- 1 cup fresh cucumber, diced
- 1 large bunch arugulas, fresh
- ¼ of a honeydew, fresh
- 1-inch piece ginger, fresh
- 1 pear, destemmed, diced
- 6 Medjool dates, pitted
- 1 tbsp sea moss gel

Directions:
1. Take a high-powered blender, switch it on, and then place all the ingredients inside, in order.
2. Close the blender, then pulses at high speed for 1 minute.

Nutrition: Calories: 329 kcal; **Protein:** 3.5 g; **Carbohydrates:** 85 g; **Fat:** 0.8 g

Dandelion and Watercress Smoothie

Preparation Time: 5 minutes

Cooking Time: 0 minute
Servings: 2
Ingredients:

- 2 cup spring water
- 1 large bunch dandelion greens, fresh
- ¼ cup key lime juice
- 1 cup watercress, fresh
- 3 baby bananas, peeled
- ½ cup fresh blueberries
- 1-inch piece ginger, fresh
- 6 Medjool dates, pitted
- 1 tbsp burdock root powder

Directions:

1. Take a high-powered blender, switch it on, and then place all the ingredients inside, in order.
2. Close the blender, then pulses at high speed for 1 minute.

Nutrition: Calories: 418.5 kcal; **Protein:** 4.2 g; **Carbohydrates:** 96.3 g; **Fat:** 1.4 g

Triple Berry Smoothie

Preparation Time: 5 minutes
Cooking Time: 0 minute
Servings: 2
Ingredients:

- 1 cup spring water
- 1 cup fresh whole strawberries
- 2 small bananas
- 1 cup fresh whole raspberries
- 2 tbsp agave syrup
- 1 cup fresh whole blueberries

Directions:

1. Take a high-powered blender, switch it on, and then place all the ingredients inside, in order.
2. Close the blender, then pulses at high speed for 1 minute.

Nutrition: Calories: 281 kcal; **Protein:** 2.8 g; **Carbohydrates:** 64.6 g; **Fat:** 1 g

28-Day Meal Plan

Day	Breakfast	Lunch	Dinner	Dessert
1	Oats with Berries	Healthy Chicken Orzo	Pan-Seared Haddock with Beets	Oats and Fruit Bar Cracker
2	Overnight Coconut Chia Oats	Quinoa With Avocado, Green Asparagus, Fresh Kelp, and Spiralized Beetroot	Paella with Chicken, Leeks, and Tarragon	Berry Blast
3	Appetizing Crepes with Berries	Fresh Tuna Steak and Fennel Salad	Chicken with Mushrooms	Apple Dumplings
4	High-Protein Breakfast Bowl	Tilapia with Limey Cilantro Salsa	Bean and Spinach Casserole	Pumpkin Peanut Pudding
5	Buckwheat Granola	Pasta with Zucchini and Peas	Caramelized Fennel and Sardines with Penne	Baked Stuffed Apples
6	Chia Pudding with Oats, Strawberries, and Kiwi	Pepper-Infused Tuna Steaks	Southwest Tofu Scramble	Carrot Cake Bites
7	Spiced Popcorn	Seared Scallops with Blood Orange Glaze	Mediterranean Turkey Breast	Papaya Cream
8	Blueberry Hemp Seed Smoothie	Broccoli with Olive Oil	Sardine Bruschetta with Fennel	Pudding Glass with Banana and Whipped Cream
9	Spiced Morning Chia Pudding	Black-Bean and Vegetable Burrito	Beans and Cucumber Salad	Apples and Cream Shake
10	Cold Oatmeal with Apple and Cinnamon	Buttered Tuna Lettuce Wraps	Lime Asparagus Spaghetti	Walnut and Oatmeal Chocolate Chip Cookies
11	Delicate Rice with Coconut and Berries	Black-Eyed Peas and Greens Power Salad	Rosemary Roasted Chicken	Healthy Chocolate Mousse

12	Vegan "Frittata"	Fish Taco Salad with Strawberry Avocado Salsa	Zucchini Noodles with Spring Vegetables	Pumpkin Pie
13	Beautiful Buckwheat Waffles	Monkfish with Sautéed Leeks, Fennel, and Zucchini	Chicken	Colorful Pops
14	Spinach Fritters	Halibut in Parchment with Zucchini, Shallots, and Herbs	Chickpea Salad	Banana Delight
15	Cucumber Bites	Sweet Life Bowl	Shrimp	Rice Pudding
16	Roasted Pumpkin Seeds	Southwestern Bean-And-Pepper Salad	Thai Chicken Thighs	Apple Couscous Pudding
17	Roasted Almonds	Simple Mediterranean Chicken	Chopped Tuna Salad	Oats and Fruit Bar Cracker
18	Gingerbread Oatmeal	Lentil-Stuffed Potato Cakes	Oven-Fried Chicken Breasts	Berry Blast
19	Granola	Roasted Chicken Thighs	White Beans with Spinach and Pan-Roasted Zucchini	Apple Dumplings
20	Spinach Avocado Smoothie	Stuffed Eggplant Shells	Honey Crusted Chicken	Pumpkin Peanut Pudding
21	High-Protein Breakfast Bowl	Sweet Potato	Artichoke and Spinach Chicken	Baked Stuffed Apples
22	Buckwheat Granola	Tofu Salad	Stuffed Chicken Breasts	Carrot Cake Bites
23	Chia Pudding with Oats, Strawberries, and Kiwi	Baked Chicken	Asparagus Cheese Vermicelli	Papaya Cream
24	Cold Oatmeal with Apple and Cinnamon	Buckwheat Tabbouleh	Zucchini and Avocado Salad	Pudding Glass with Banana and Whipped Cream

25	Delicate Rice with Coconut and Berries	Southwestern Chicken and Pasta	Feta Zucchini Salad	Apples and Cream Shake
26	Vegan "Frittata"	Pepper Chicken	Chickpea Butternut Squash	Walnut and Oatmeal Chocolate Chip Cookies
27	Beautiful Buckwheat Waffles	Loaded Baked Sweet Potatoes	Mustard Chicken Tenders	Pumpkin Pie
28	Appetizing Crepes with Berries	Coriander and Mint With Turmeric Roasted Cauliflower	Apricot Chicken	Colorful Pops

Measurement Conversion Chart

Volume Equivalents (Liquid)

US Standard	US Standard (oz.)	Metric (approximate)
2 tbsp	1 fl. oz.	30 mL
¼ cup	2 fl. oz.	60 mL
½ cup	4 fl. oz.	120 mL
1 cup	8 fl. oz.	240 mL
1½ cups	12 fl. oz.	355 mL
2 cups or 1 pint	16 fl. oz.	475 mL
4 cups or 1 quart	32 fl. oz.	1 L
gallon	128 fl. oz.	4 L

Volume Equivalents (Dry)

US Standard	Metric (approximate)
⅛ tsp	0.5 mL
¼ tsp	1 mL
½ tsp	2 mL
¾ tsp	4 mL
1 tsp	5 mL
1 tbsp	15 mL
¼ cup	59 mL
⅓ cup	79 mL
½ cup	118 mL
⅔ cup	156 mL
¾ cup	177 mL
1 cup	235 mL
2 cups or 1 pint	475 mL
3 cups	700 mL
4 cups or 1 quart	1 L

Oven Temperatures

Fahrenheit (F)	Celsius (C)
250°F	120°C
300°F	150°C
325°F	165°C
50°F	180°C
375°F	190°C
400°F	200°C
425°F	220°C
450°F	230°C

Weight Equivalents

US Standard	Metric
½ oz.	1g
1 oz.	3g
2 oz.	6g
4 oz.	11g
8 oz.	22g
12 oz.	34g
16 oz. or 1 lb.	45g

Conclusion

Managing gastroesophageal reflux disease (GERD) through diet and lifestyle changes can be an effective way to reduce symptoms and improve overall health. By focusing on foods that are low in acid, avoiding foods and beverages that are known to aggravate GERD symptoms, eating smaller, more frequent meals, and maintaining a healthy weight, individuals with GERD can find relief and improve their quality of life.

This book has provided a variety of delicious and nutritious recipes that are suitable for those with GERD. From breakfast to dinner, and even snacks and desserts, these recipes are designed to be easy to prepare and enjoyable to eat. They also include a range of ingredients that are known to be beneficial for GERD, such as ginger, chamomile, and licorice.

In addition, this book has provided information on lifestyle changes, such as avoiding eating close to bedtime and regular exercise, that can also help to reduce GERD symptoms.

Remember that everyone's GERD experience is unique, and what works for someone may not work for someone else. It is usually preferable to get personalized guidance from a healthcare practitioner or a nutritionist. With the right diet and lifestyle changes, however, individuals with GERD can find relief and improve their quality of life.

We are sure that the Recipes proposed in this cookbook will help you to improve your health and live a happier life.

The greatest gift you can give your family and the world is a healthy you!

Made in the USA
Monee, IL
01 May 2023

32741910R00061